THE ANNOTATED SHAKESPEARE

Hamlet

William Shakespeare

Fully annotated, with an Introduction, by Burton Raffel

With an essay by Harold Bloom

THE ANNOTATED SHAKESPEARE

Burton Raffel, General Editor

Yale University Press • *New Haven and London*

Designed by Rebecca Gibb
Set in Bembo type by The Composing Room of Michigan, Inc.
Printed in the United States of America by R. R. Donnelley & Sons.

Library of Congress Cataloging-in-Publication Data
Shakespeare, William, 1564–1616.
Hamlet / William Shakespeare ; fully annotated, with an introduction by
Burton Raffel ; with an essay by Harold Bloom.
p.   cm.
Includes bibliographical references.
ISBN 0-300-10105-8 (paperbound)
ISBN 0-300-10175-9 (cloth)
1. Hamlet (Legendary character)—Drama.   2. Murder victims'
families—Drama.   3. Fathers—Death—Drama.   4. Princes—Drama.
5. Revenge—Drama.   6. Denmark—Drama.   I. Raffel, Burton.
II. Bloom, Harold.   III. Title.
PR2807.A2R34 2003
822.3′3—dc21
2003005805

A catalogue record for this book is available from the British Library.

10 9 8 7 6 5 4 3

For my four sisters: Catherine, Teresa, Joan, and Martha

CONTENTS

About This Book ix

Introduction xv

The Tragedy of Hamlet, Prince of Denmark 1

An Essay by Harold Bloom 229

Further Reading 245

Finding List 249

ABOUT THIS BOOK

Written four centuries ago, in a fairly early form of Modern English, *Hamlet* is a notoriously dense, complex text of remarkable depth and beauty. Many of the play's social and historical underpinnings necessarily need explanation for the modern reader. But what needs even more, and far more detailed, explanation are the very words.

'A did comply with his dug, before 'a sucked it. Thus has he, and many more of the same bevy that I know the drossy age dotes on, only got the tune of the time and, out of a habit of encounter, a kind of yeasty collection, which carries them through and through the most fanned and winnowed opinions. And do but blow them to their trial, the bubbles are out.

This is Hamlet himself, in act 5, scene 2, speaking to his friend and companion, Horatio, about Osric, an outrageously fashionable courtier who has just left them. Hamlet is profoundly disgusted by Osric's speech and behavior. But in the most basic of all senses of "meaning," what is this fiercely contemptuous speech all about? What is it (what are its words) *saying?* Longtime scholars of Elizabethan literature have learned to fully understand; they delight in teaching the play to those less well learned. But what can the unlearned, trying to read *Hamlet,* make of what surely often seems to them, in passages like that just quoted, a kind of weirdly surrealistic jumble?

> *Hamlet.* 'A[1] did comply[2] with his dug,[3] before 'a sucked it. Thus has he, and many more of the same bevy[4] that I know the drossy[5] age dotes on, only got[6] the tune[7] of the time and, out of an habit of encounter,[8] a kind of yeasty collection,[9] which carries them through and through[10] the most fanned and winnowed[11] opinions. And do but blow them to their trial,[12] the bubbles are out.[13]

I believe annotations of this sort create the necessary bridges from Shakespeare's four-centuries-old English across to ours. The only "difficult" word I have not explained is "dote"; the omission is deliberate. Many readers new to matters Elizabethan will already understand this still-current, and largely unchanged, word. "Tune,"

1 he
2 observe the formalities of politeness
3 the nipple of his nurse's breast
4 company, crowd (primarily used with reference to women)
5 scum-filled, rubbish-ridden
6 "only got" = "have/have acquired/caught only"
7 style, frame of mind
8 "an habit of encounter" = "a settled/habitual/rote way of face-to-face meeting"
9 "yeasty collection" = "fermenting/restlessly turbid/frothy/foaming collection/summary/abstract"
10 "through and through" = "from beginning to end, over and over again"
11 "fanned and winnowed" = "(long since) thoroughly blown about and sifted"
12 examination, test, proof
13 popped, extinguished

meaning "melody," is of course a word familiar to all speakers of the language. But its sense, here, "style, frame of mind," will not similarly be clear. The same is true of such familiar expressions as "only got" and "through and through." Some readers, to be sure, will comprehend their unusual, historical meanings without glosses. And when it comes to words like "dote," those who are not familiar with the modern meaning will easily find a clear, simple definition in any modern dictionary. And they may be obliged to make fairly frequent use of such a dictionary: there are a good many words, in *Hamlet,* to be found in modern dictionaries and not glossed here. But there are just as surely readers who will not understand Shakespeare's intended meaning, absent such glosses as I here offer. And it seems to me my editorial responsibility to guarantee as complete verbal accessibility as I am able to provide. I followed the same principle in compiling *The Annotated Milton,* published in 1999, and classroom experience has validated that decision. Classes of mixed upper-level undergraduates and graduate students have more quickly and thoroughly transcended language barriers than ever before. This allows the teacher to move more promptly and confidently to the nonlinguistic matters that have made Milton a great and important poet. Shakespeare's language is more or less equally difficult. No one who has not understood the *words* of *Hamlet* can either fully or properly come to grips with the imperishable matter of the play.

Not all of *Hamlet* will appear so impenetrable. But the inevitable forces of linguistic change, operant in all living tongues, have inevitably created wide degrees of obstacles to ready comprehension—not only sharply different meanings but subtle, partial shifts in meaning which allow us to think that we understand when, alas, we do not. Speakers of Dutch and German, too, experience this shifting of the linguistic ground. Like Early Modern English (ca. 1600) and the Modern English now current, those languages are too close for those who know only one language, and not the other, to be able readily to recognize just what they correctly understand and what they do not. In the very first scene of *Hamlet,* for example, when the sentry Francisco directs Barnardo, arriving on the castle's guard platform in the darkness of night, to "Stand and unfold yourself," we can pretty reasonably guess what "unfold" might have meant, in Shakespeare's time. To make things both plain and definite, however, I have in this edition glossed "unfold" as "reveal, disclose, identify," giving the neophyte modern reader the security of certainty as well as what is I think a useful sense of the word's range, in Shakespeare's time. But I have also glossed "stand," because it is precisely the sort of misleading "false friend" I have been talking about. It does not in fact mean what we mean by "stand," which is "stand up" as opposed to "sit down." Rather, it means "halt, stop"—which might perhaps be guessed at, but equally well might not even be noticed by a modern reader, who knows perfectly well what "stand" means to him or her.

I have sometimes annotated prosody (metrics), though only when that has seemed truly necessary or particularly helpful. My standard for the few prosodic usages I have glossed is not so much ad hoc as it is founded both in long experience in the classroom (I taught my first university class in fall 1948) and my clear perception of a powerful paradigm shift in general literacy. Books have been, not surprisingly, the place where people have learned to read. It seems to me apparent that for almost a century books have been losing that position, being to a significant extent replaced first by movies and now, even more meaningfully, by a variety of electronically generated screens. Inevitably, those screens are heavily visual and minimally language-oriented. This is not the place to descant on such subjects, but the subtitle of my essay "Freshman Decomposition" seems to me to say what needs saying: "not the same freshmen." (The essay appears in *Palo Alto Review*, Fall 2001.) In glossing prosody, as in glossing words, I believe we have no choice but to deal with the students we actually have, not with the largely no longer extant students we either once had or deeply wish we still had. It is my belief that we will not have such students again.

The notation used in discussing prosody, as in indicating pronunciation, follows the extremely simple form used in my *From Stress to Stress: An Autobiography of English Prosody* (see "Further Reading," near the end of this book). Syllables with metrical stress are capitalized; all other syllables are in lowercase.

I have annotated, as well, a limited number of such other matters, sometimes of interpretation, sometimes of general or historical relevance, as have seemed to me seriously worthy of inclusion. These annotations have been most carefully restricted: this is not a book of literary commentary. It is for that reason that the glossing of metaphors has been severely restricted. There is almost literally no end to discussion and/or analysis of metaphor, especially in Shakespeare. To yield to temptation might well be to double or triple the size of this book—and would also change it from a historically oriented language guide to a work of an unsteadily mixed nature. In the process, I believe, neither language nor literature would be well or clearly served.

In the interests of compactness and brevity, I have employed in my annotations (as consistently as I am able) a number of stylistic and typographical devices:

- Words or phrases separated by either a comma or a forward slash (/) are supplementary to one another. I have used the former sign in brief (usually one- or two-word) annotations, and the latter sign in longer annotations.

- Alternative but complementary meanings are usually indicated by *and;* contrasting meanings by *or;* and meanings that might be both complementary and contrasting by *and/or.* These meanings are placed in parentheses, to highlight them for the reader. Instances of special interest are set off with lowercase arabic numerals, (1), (2), and so on.

- Except for proper nouns, the word at the beginning of all annotations is in lowercase.

- Unresolved uncertainties are followed by a question mark, set in parentheses (?). Textual differences have been annotated only when the differences seem either marked or of unusual interest.

- Annotations of more common words have not been repeated. The note annotating the first instance of more common words is followed by the sign ★. Readers may easily track down the first annotation, using the brief "Finding List" at the back of the book.

- When particularly relevant, "translations" into twenty-first-century English have been added, in parentheses.

The most important typographical device here employed is ★ placed after the first (and only) gloss of words and phrases very frequently used in Hamlet. I have provided an alphabetically arranged listing of such words and phrases in the "Finding List" at the back of the book. This distinctly telegraphic listing contains no annotations—simply the words or phrases themselves and the page and note numbers, where the annotation of the words or phrases can be found.

INTRODUCTION

History is littered with "solutions" to the ineffable, entrancing, will-o'-the-wisp "meaning" of *Hamlet*. Perhaps the most charming of all was that of the delightfully insane fellow, who shall here go nameless, so convinced that the answer to the perpetual puzzle lay hidden under the stones in Elsinore castle—and he knew just which stones, too—that he persuaded the benevolent Danes to let him turn over exactly those stones, still lying quietly in place after all these centuries. He turned them over, one by one. And he looked. And what he found was dust, and dirt, and a few bugs.

No one, I think, can or ever will "solve" *Hamlet*. In the first of the three sections that follow, I want to discuss the pre-history of the play—or, more exactly, what we know and what we do not know about that history. It has, as I shall explain, a profound relevance for puzzling out the meaning of what William Shakespeare wrote. In the second section, I want to discuss aspects of the play's two chief characters, Hamlet and Ophelia. There is no need to set out even the general range of more than three hundred years of proposed "solutions." The earlier period is neatly recorded, with generous (and quite fascinating) excerpts in Horace Howard Furness's 1877 Variorum Edition. Modern criticism is summarized and analyzed, with remarkable objectivity, in Gottschalk's 1972 study. In the third and last section of this Introduction, I will briefly discuss textual sources and the editorial principles responsible for the text of the play as here presented.

The Pre-History of Hamlet

The first link in the Hamlet story is the likely but unprovable assumption that, at some distant and unknown time, a bloody family feud much like other bloody family feuds occurred somewhere in Scandinavia. Storytelling was without question a prime art, in all ancient heroic societies, and Scandinavia (from Iceland all the way across to Finland) developed some of the world's finest tales. (We know most of them under the general heading of "sagas.") The particular blood feud that began the Hamlet story, however, had a rather special twist of high fictive interest. The central figure was seeking revenge against an uncle who had murdered the young man's father, who was also the murderer's brother. Too powerless to be able, as yet, to effect that revenge, the young man sought refuge, successfully, in pretended madness.

Amhlaide is how Hamlet was named, in the next link in the story, which is also our first written record of the principal character's name, though not yet of the tale proper. We do not have a whole work, but only a fragmentary mention in still another account, Snorri Sturluson's *Prose Edda,* dated to ca. 1230. Snorri's mention of Amhlaide attributes it to what he tells us us is an Irish lament, probably of the tenth century A.D. Clearly, the name Amhlaide is a Celtic adaptation, based on a Scandinavian original. In this lament, put into the mouth of a mourning widow, Amh-

laide is described as a Dane, and as the killer, in a historically ver-
ified battle that took place in 919, of the widow's husband, a king
named Niall. This first documentary record indicates the living
nature of the Hamlet tale, though without further knowledge of
the lament itself we have no idea of exactly what its narrative nature may have been. Nor do we know what the general shape of
the Hamlet tale proper then was, or whether it took something
like its later form first in Ireland or after it had been exported
back to Scandinavia. Plainly, however, there had been an exporta-
tion of the tale to Ireland, whatever form it may have taken: this
was yet another link in the haze-filled background of the Hamlet
tale. Stories of no large inherent interest do not travel well. This
one obviously did.

But by the time of the next link in the story's development,
datable to Denmark and to the early thirteenth century, we can
see that the Hamlet story has advanced a large step toward Shakespeare's play. An ecclesiastic in the service of a Danish bishop,
Saxo Grammaticus (ca. 1150–1216), compiled a *Historia* (or *Gesta*)
Danica, "Stories/Deeds of the Danes." Saxo wrote in Latin; he may
have been working from assorted sources also in Latin, though we
do not know. Now we are given a prince, Amletha, whose father,
the king of Denmark, was murdered by his brother, Fengo. Fengo
then married his brother's widow, Gerutha. Fengo plainly meant
to finish his capture of the throne by murdering Amletha, but the
prince pretended insanity (one did not, could not, kill the mad)
and produced a veritable storm of crazed acts to verify his in-
vented but protective madness. He would throw himself into
muck and rub filth all over his face and clothes. Taken to a forest
by his uncle's men, to test his sanity more closely, Amletha was
careful to mount his horse backwards, setting the reins on the

horse's tail. Confronted by an apparently amorous young woman, set in his way at his uncle's command, Amletha avoids this trap, too, eventually making the hard-pressed young woman (the germ of the character we know as Ophelia) his comrade, though not his lover.

There is the germ of the character we know as Polonius, too. A friend of Fengo's more subtly tempts Amletha, using the young man's mother as bait. The friend is hidden in the mother's chambers, lying under a pile of straw. Amletha acts out his "madness" by leaping and jumping and thrashing, and—the moment he "accidentally" discovers a "lump" in the straw—Amletha stabs the king's friend to death. Fengo questions Amletha and is told a fanciful (but essentially truthful) story of the friend falling into the castle's privy sewer. After having drowned in its filth and ordure, reports Amletha craftily, he was finally found and eaten by pigs. By this time exceedingly suspicious of his nephew, Fengo ships Amletha off to England, accompanied by two courtiers. The Danish king's message to the English king is direct and simple: kill Amletha. On the voyage, as in Shakespeare's play, Amletha steals the escorts' documents and substitutes his own, which now ask the English king to kill the escorts.

But neither Amletha nor his escorts are promptly killed. And here the story veers sharply from the tale we know. Amletha becomes a sort of prophet to the English king, then becomes the husband of the king's daughter, and, as a result, his escorts are indeed hanged. A year later, Amletha returns to Denmark and, after a renewed masquerade of madness, kills Fengo and assumes the throne himself.

Saxo's story is brutal and blunt. Many of its details, and a good deal of its narrative, are totally unlike Shakespeare's tale, and there is little subtlety. Other writers subsequently mentioned and sometimes adapted Saxo; we need not examine them, since there is no evidence whatever that either Shakespeare or the writer of the next and final pre-Shakespearean link ever did.

This all-important link in the Hamlet story, alas, is lost, apparently beyond recall. It is an earlier Elizabethan play, approximately datable because it was sharply criticized in 1589 by Thomas Nash (1567–1601). The title of this play was *Hamlet*. We do not know how long it had at that point been on the Elizabethan stage; we do not know for certain who was its author, though circumstantial evidence favors the melodramatist, Thomas Kyd (1558–94), a friend to both Christopher Marlowe and the young Shakespeare. Most seriously of all, we do not have so much as a fragment of this play's text, nor do we know how it handled the old tale. Knowing what we do of Kyd's surviving work, and also from what we learn in the documentation on his arrest, in 1593, first on the grounds of public libel and, subsequently, on the added and much more serious charge of blasphemy (he was imprisoned, tortured, and finally cleared, though he died just a year and a half after his release), we can perhaps speculate, though only vaguely, about what his *Hamlet*—if it was indeed his—"must" have been like. But these seem to me fundamentally empty speculations: the "must-have-beens" of history, like the dews of morning, tend to evaporate under our breath, as we lean close and try to make ingenious use of them. In matters textual, literary, and above all verbal, ingenuity is no substitute for reality.

How much of the many "alterations" in Shakespeare's retelling of the old story come from the old play, or from his own fertile imagination, or from sources of which we have no knowledge, it is therefore quite impossible to say. And as if the picture was not muddied enough, there is yet another stage to be accounted for, as best we can, in this pre-history of *Hamlet*. Once again, there is no exactitude in the dating, but at some point after 1598 Shakespeare appears to have been called upon, as he more than likely often was (being a "house" dramatist), to "update" the lost predecessor-*Hamlet*. That play had been very popular; Shakespeare's company owned the "rights"; and so good a "property" fairly called for exploitation. We do not know how long thereafter Shakespeare decided, if he did decide, or was asked, to entirely re-do the old play (if—and we do not know for sure—that was what he did in the end do). In a remark more or less datable to the period 1599–1601, Gabriel Harvey (good friend of Edmund Spenser) noted the popularity of "Shakespeare's . . . tragedie of Hamlet, Prince of Denmarke . . ." Was this a reference to a revision, or to a "new" version? Shakespeare's own *Hamlet* seems to have been on the Elizabethan stage by 1602, when an apparent reference was made to it by George Chapman and, still more concretely, a prepublication notice was filed, describing it as having been "latelie Acted by the Chamberleyne his servantes," this being a reference to Shakespeare's company (transformed, somewhat later, into the "King's company").

An apparently pirated edition, now known as the First Quarto (a reference to page size and binding style), appeared in 1603. It is clearly what is called a "bad quarto," though even a bad text can be made use of, in formulating editorial decisions. In 1604, fairly clearly in response to the distinctly mangled First Quarto, appeared the Second Quarto, almost twice the length and, it is agreed, a much fairer representation of the play. Reprintings of the latter occurred, until finally, in 1623, the Folio edition was printed, apparently from a manuscript source—though no one knows whether this was Shakespeare's manuscript or (since he had died in 1616), more probably, one owned by his company. Again, there is no way of knowing. The Folio text is the longest of all; it is however not carefully, accurately printed. Textual editors are obliged, accordingly, to work back and forth between it and the Second Quarto, occasionally turning to the First Quarto, in order to arrive as closely as possible to Shakespeare's text. That process is still going on. How close any modern text actually is to what Shakespeare wrote, or to the final state of what he wrote, remains a matter of continued examination and dispute. There is no manuscript material, absolutely nothing in Shakespeare's own hand.

My procedure, since this an edition primarily intended for use in schools and colleges, and secondarily by those not attending school and desiring more textual help than anything but an annotated edition can supply, has been as follows: I have focused bilaterally, on one hand making use of the three seventeenth-century sources just described, and on the other consulting those modern editions most widely in use. My desire is to include in my finished text everything that, after consideration of the (forever inconclusive) evidence, is likely to have been written by Shakespeare. Fairly extensive passages have been drawn from the Second Quarto, because the probably more authoritative Folio omits them. Transcription and typesetting errors abound in all the play's sources, as they usually do in seventeenth-century printed books. To reach a conflated, consensus edition involves constant checking, back and forth, in order to produced a unified, historically sensible text. For the reader's enlightenment, I have footnoted my most severely difficult choices.

A "perfect text" remains an impossibility—not something

hard to attain, but something forever out of the question. Indeed, editors have sometimes assumed the existence of two quite distinct and somehow equally authoritative Shakespearian *Hamlets,* or even three, and united them in one volume, as individually distinct reading texts. This seems to me to destroy rather than enhance reading—much like laying out the basic linguistic and cultural elements of a work written in a language other than English and declaring, "Reader, I stop here. These are your essential materials, the stuff from which the literary work you propose to read was in fact constructed. Now that you have these materials, you are on your own. Proceed, therefore, to shape this disassembled book by Zola, or Tolstoy, or Homer, as you please." E. Talbot Donaldson introduces his *prose* translation of the *Beowulf poem* in exactly these terms: "Rather than create a new and lesser poem for the reader, it seems better to offer him in prose the literal materials from which he can re-create the poem" (Norton Critical Edition, xvi).

But we are none of us Shakespeare any more than we are Emile Zola or Leo Tolstoy or the *Beowulf* poet. Breaking *Hamlet* into what we as editors think are its component parts, and then presenting each of those parts, can be useful to scholars, and to other editors. But it is the exact opposite of what I here try to offer—a cohesive, sensible and unitary text, about as close to what Shakespeare actually wrote as, alas, we are ever going to get. I see no point, from the perspective of the common reader, or the student, to deliberately de-composing Shakespeare's play.

The Roles of Hamlet and Ophelia

One of the great theatrical directors of the twentieth century, Konstantin Stanislavsky, said in 1938 that being called upon to play the lead role in *Hamlet* remained (he was addressing theater people) the "greatest stumbling block in our profession" (*Shakespeare in the Soviet Union,* 148). What other male lead role has been played, over the years, by so many world-famous actresses—among others, Sarah Siddons, in the eighteenth century; Sarah Bernhardt, in the nineteenth century; Judith Anderson and Eva Le Galliene, in the twentieth century? In addition to the characterological difficulties (and attractions) of the role, however, there are important structural aspects, as well.

The characters of *Hamlet* are deftly realized. We as audience (or readers: Charles Lamb famously declared that the play should *only* be read, for it was impossible ever to stage it) are always aware, precisely and clearly, of what we need to know in order to keep the dramatic action in motion. But the dimensions of the characters vary immensely, and only two—Hamlet and Ophelia—seem to me deeply three-dimensional. That is, Claudius, Polonius, Laertes, Horatio, Rosencrantz and Guildenstern, and the many lesser personages are solidly founded, consistent, totally functional. In theater terminology, they hold the stage, they *work*. (The latter must also be said of Gertrude, though in my judgment her portrayal is less convincing as a whole.) There needs to be no particular mystery attached to these characters, nor is there. The greater mystery is of course Hamlet; the lesser and rather neglected (or misperceived) mystery is Ophelia. And the actors portraying these latter two roles are inevitably put in the position of having to deal with, to represent, to make dramatically functional, what is in the end not quite representable.

My 1996 essay, "Hamlet and the Tradition of the Novel," deals with this from a literary rather than from a dramatic perspective. Let me initially approach the problem, here, from a heavily actor-oriented viewpoint. Although Hamlet makes a lessened appearance on stage, in the fourth of the play's five acts, he is nevertheless by a rough count on stage (usually but not always with other characters) during 66 percent of a performance of the full text. No other character in the play comes close to this large a stage presence. His solo appearances, of course, in his justly famous monologues, are both a special dramatic challenge and a magnificent dramatic opportunity. Ophelia, indeed, appears only 17 percent of the time, and never alone. Hamlet's is a strikingly large on-stage presence, especially juxtaposed against similarly derived estimates for some of the others among Shakespeare's more famous plays. In *King Lear,* Lear himself is on stage roughly 48 percent of the time, and never alone. Othello is on stage 59 percent of the time (and never alone)—but he is not, at least in these terms, the major figure in his play, for Iago is on stage roughly 64 percent of the time. And the play's famous monologues belong exclusively to Iago. Macbeth appears almost exactly as often as does Othello, but he, too, with characters having on-stage presences very nearly as powerful, namely Lady Macbeth and Macduff, who appear, respectively, roughly 30 percent and 25 percent of the time. Not only do all three have solo moments on-stage, but so, too, do two other characters, Banquo and, at the play's close, Malcolm. Even soaringly preeminent Prospero, in *The Tempest,* appears roughly 52 percent of the time, and once again shares the stage with Ariel, at 31 percent, Miranda, at 27 percent, and Caliban, at 25 percent. Prospero, like Hamlet, has solo appearances, but so, too, does Caliban. (Note, too, that while *The Tempest* is a fairly short play, *Hamlet* is Shakespeare's longest.) Finally, in a late problem play of more or less the same date as *Hamlet* (1604), *Measure for Measure,* we find a distinctly even-handed sharing of on-stage time: Isabella and the Duke both are to be seen roughly 44 percent of the time, and Angelo 30 percent. All of these figures are no more than approximations, but they are similarly derived and at least comparable, each to the other. And they emphatically support and emphasize Hamlet's massive performance visibility.

We do not know, once again, why Hamlet hesitates as he does. If we speculate that he is neurotically unable to act, what do we do with his instantaneous dispatching of Polonius or his brilliantly and promptly executed counterplot, in defeating the King's plan to have his patently dangerous nephew executed immediately upon his landing in England? If we speculate that Hamlet is in love with Ophelia, because he at some points says he is (and what's more was so all along), how do we deal with his express disclaimers and his clear indication, after the fact, that his graveside declamation of eternal love for her was provoked by Laertes' ridiculously overblown rhetoric, just before? If Hamlet is the tool, for better or worse, of the Ghost, and spurred by his burning desire to revenge the father-figure that the Ghost says he is, how can it be that, in the final scene, Hamlet does not attack the King, even after his mother's death, until after he learns that he himself, like Laertes (who informs him of the plot), has been fatally poisoned? As he rushes at the King, he *still* advances no explanation for so doing other than his own poisoning. Only when the King, seriously wounded, appeals for help, claiming not to be mortally hurt, does the by-now thoroughly aroused Hamlet declare that Claudius is "incestuous [and] murd'rous," adding, in his fury, that Claudius is also "damnèd," hardly in truth a revenge issue. Hamlet is a marvelously witty man: even in his most "maddened" moments, he sparks off puns and bright words like the word-loving human volcano he is. What is it he has visibly lost, in his so-called madness—which he himself tells us, as he tells Horatio, is faked—other than his garters, his hairbrush, and whatever concern he has previously displayed for others, notably Ophelia and his mother, the Queen?

The questions, the puzzles, can be further prolonged. But the actor representing Hamlet must persuade us at every point that his character's actions are authentic—not so much "realistic," for the Elizabethan stage is not that of George Bernard Shaw, but *true*. And true, that is, in terms of the conventions and dramatic realities of Shakespeare's stage, not ours. I do not find it possible to doubt Shakespeare, who is at his superb best in this play. Nor is it simply his utterly magnificent ability to deploy the English language that so completely persuades me, as it has been persuading people for the four centuries of the play's glowing, brilliant existence. "The play's the thing," says Hamlet, and indeed it is. The play is totally convincing—but of what? "Ay, there's the rub," as Hamlet also says.

Ophelia has been misperceived, I think, but not from authorial prejudice against women (which in my judgment is not to be found in Shakespeare). Rather, Ophelia has been misperceived because insufficient attention has been paid to her character according to the standards of *her* time, rather than ours. She is as I have said on stage less than 20 percent of the time; it is thus neither difficult nor wearying to trace the complete outline of her characterization, appearance by appearance.

We first meet Ophelia in act 1, scene 3, when Laertes, about to take sail for France, says farewell to her. She is young, female, formally restricted in many ways by custom and habit to a more or less semi-subservient role—but her very first words to her brother tell us that here is a humble maiden with a difference. "Let me hear from you," says her brother. Does Ophelia tamely, servilely agree? Not a bit of it. "Do you doubt that?" she throws back at him. He tells her at great length, and in conventionally masculine language, to be wary of Hamlet, ending, "No more." Does she accept his distinctly condescending words? "No more but so?" she challenges. He then launches into almost thirty-five lines of "more," to which she responds with seven terse, forth-right lines well worth quoting in full: "I shall the effect of this good lesson [mere politeness? Laertes is not very bright and does not ever say much worth remembering] keep / As watchman to my heart. But, good my brother, / Do not, as some ungracious pastors do, / Show me the steep and thorny way to heaven, / Whiles, like a puffed and reckless libertine, / Himself the prim-rose path of dalliance treads, / And recks not his own rede." For a supposedly timid, obsequious female, this is remarkably blunt—and would, I have little doubt, have been so perceived by contem-porary audiences. For Ophelia and Laertes represent, as so often in Shakespeare, a pointed pair in carefully set contrast, he the bold-talking male, she the obviously brainier, necessarily re-strained but at the same time distinctly unimpressed female.

Ophelia is necessarily much less free of her speech, in the fol-lowing exchanges with her father. According to the conventions of Shakespeare's time, a brother does not exercise the same dis-positive power over a younger, female sibling that a father wields (though once a father dies, the brother, absent a husband, assumes a paternalistic role). "I do not know, my lord," Ophelia quite properly tells her father, "what I should think." Polonius is brusque and lordly with her. She does not, however, simply crum-ple, nor does she fawn. "My lord," she tells him, "he hath impor-tuned me with love / In honorable fashion." Her father is scornful. "And [he has] given countenance to his speech, my lord," she presses on, "With almost all the holy vows of heaven." Her father harangues her at length and she bows, as in the end she and the audience know she must, with a simple "I shall obey, my lord."

In act 2, scene 1, she rushes to her father, frightened and understandably dismayed by Hamlet's wild behavior and appearance. "O my lord, my lord, I have been so affrighted." She proceeds to tells all: Hamlet has appeared before her, looking "as if he had been loosèd out of hell / To speak of horrors." "Did you cause this, he demands? "No, my good lord," she says. "But as you did command, / I did repel his letters and denied / His access to me." She is at no point obsequious, but she is, nevertheless, a sequestered, inexperienced girl. There are serious questions, as I have said, about Hamlet's love for her. There do not seem to be any such questions about her love for him—and his sudden wild appearance *ought* under all the circumstances to be frightening.

We do not next see Ophelia until act 3, scene 1, in which after a polite pair of brief speeches by her and a pair of abrupt, unpleasant ones from Hamlet—the second one denying ever making presents to her—she confronts him, quietly but firmly: "My honored lord, you know right well you did, / And with them words of so sweet breath composed / As made the things more rich. Their perfume lost, / Take these again, for to the noble mind / Rich gifts wax poor when givers prove unkind. / There, my lord." And she hands him back his presents, obliging him thereby to grudgingly accept them. This is clearly forceful in both language and action. Hamlet continues his rude, abrupt speech, but Ophelia still meets him ably, matching him on his own high standard of eloquent argument. (He has been trained in a university; she of course has not.) "Could beauty, my lord, have better com-

merce than with honesty?" Hamlet admits, "I did love you once."
Her response, once again, is direct and stalwart: "Indeed, my lord,
you made me believe so." He reprimands her for having believed
him. She is sadly but bravely up to this retort, too: "I was the more
deceived." As Hamlet works himself into an apparent (?) fit, she
grows desperate—for it is as I have noted plain that she has loved
him all along. "O, help him, you sweet heavens!" she cries, and
then, "O heavenly powers, restore him!" These, too, are not the
speeches of a feeble-willed woman; their agitation is easy both to
understand and to appreciate. And when at last Hamlet storms
out, she speaks twelve nobly mournful lines, ending: "O, woe is
me, / T'have seen what I have seen, see what I see!" Where is
the weakness in any of this?

Later in scene 2 of the same act, Hamlet sprawls next to her, as
they watch the play within a play. She meets his overexcited
repartee with dignified, courteous cordiality. When he asks if she
thinks he is talking "dirty" to her, she replies only, "I think nothing, my lord." He wisecracks on: "you are merry, my lord," she
observes. When he (deliberately?) mistakes how long ago his father died, she quietly corrects him. When the play within a play
begins, he comments liberally, and very freely; she patiently dis-
avows his remarks: "You are naught [wicked, naughty], you are
naught. I'll mark [pay attention to] the play." Later, she remarks, as
he chatters on, "You are as good as a chorus, my lord," she tells him.
"You are keen, my lord, you are keen." As he waxes both witty and
bawdy, and becomes explicitly licentious (in speech, at least), she
turns it and him away with "Still better, and worse." Hers is, in
short, a sturdy, sane, courageous stand under very heavy male fire.

Hamlet kills her father; Ophelia, deeply shaken, unravels. Act
4, scene 5, her mad scene, does not show us the same young

woman earlier and consistently encountered. Is this anything but a sadly appropriate response from a young woman of Shakespeare's time, not of ours, deprived, first, of the man she loves and then of her father? (For whatever use he might be in these circumstances, her brother is abroad.) Ophelia's world has been shaken, and then it has been cracked. There is, for her and for other Elizabethan women in similar circumstances, no pathway out of despair and hopelessness. As Horatio says of Hamlet, immediately after his death, "Now cracks a noble heart." In Shakespeare's time, as in ours and all other times, the paths of men and women do not often run in exactly the same directions, except to the common graves that hold us all.

This Text

As I have said, I present, here, a conservative and consensual text of the play. I have not followed any single seventeenth-century or any modern text, but in a sense I have followed all of them. That is, there is no radical departure, in this edition, from what seem to me the agreed-upon editorial standards of this time, most especially in the United States. Choices, of course, have had to be made, and I have made them, using the textual resources cited in "Further Reading," at the end of this book. I have carefully consulted those resources. I have however not noted each and every such choice, but only those that seem, for one reason or another, particularly worth attention in an edition meant primarily for nonscholar readers.

I have been free only with what might be called the lesser and more mechanical aspects of the play. As in virtually all modern editions, I have modernized spelling, except where that might in-

terfere with Shakespeare's prosody. Final *-ed* is given an accent—
è—when, and *only* when, *-ed* is syllabified. Absence of that accent
mark indicates nonsyllabification. There are in a few cases accent
marks on other words, once again for prosodic reasons.

I have repunctuated wherever I thought it necessary, and
sometimes reparagraphed. I have added occasional minor stage
directions, mostly indications for the general reader as to just who
is speaking to whom. There is no firm Elizabethan standard in any
of these matters, though I have tried to be as respectful as possible
of what is to be found in the early-seventeenth-century texts of
Hamlet. Elizabethan printers cannot be equated with modern
ones. Neither can the standards of modern authorship be retro-
actively applied to writers who did not, in the modern sense of
the word, consider themselves to be "authors."

Having many times taught this play, and many others by
Shakespeare, my single goal has been to make an edition that
readers and, in particular, students (and students at all levels) will
find as fully accessible as this somewhat disordered early-seventeenth-century text can be faithfully made.

The Tragedy of

Hamlet

PRINCE OF DENMARK

CHARACTERS (DRAMATIS PERSONAE)

Hamlet (Prince of Denmark)

Claudius (King of Denmark, Hamlet's uncle, brother of the recently dead King)

Ghost (Hamlet's father, the former King)

Gertrude (Hamlet's mother, now married to Claudius)

Polonius (councillor/adviser to the King)

Laertes (Polonius's son)

Ophelia (Polonius's daughter)

Horatio (friend, companion, and fellow-student of Hamlet)

Rosencrantz and Guildenstern (fellow-students and former friends of Hamlet)

Fortinbras (Prince of Norway. N.B.: just as Hamlet's father is also named Hamlet, so Fortinbras's father, too, is named Fortinbras)

Voltemand and Cornelius (Danish councillors, ambassadors to Norway)

Marcellus, Barnardo, Francisco (members of the King's guard)

Osric (a singularly foppish courtier)

Reynaldo (Polonius's servant)

Players (actors)

Gentlemen (courtiers)

Priest

Clown 1 and Clown 2 (gravediggers)

Captain (in the army led by Fortinbras)

English ambassadors (to Denmark)

Others

Act I

—⊷⊶⊷—

The castle, in Elsinore: a guard platform—that is, a raised surface

ENTER (AT OPPOSITE ENDS OF THE STAGE) BARNARDO
AND FRANCISCO, TWO SENTINELS

Barnardo Who's there?

Francisco Nay, answer me. Stand and ~~unfold~~[1] yourself.

Barnardo Long live the king![2]

Francisco Barnardo?

Barnardo He.   5

Francisco You come most carefully[3] upon your hour.[4]

Barnardo 'Tis now struck twelve. Get thee to bed, Francisco.

Francisco For this relief much thanks: 'tis bitter cold,
    And I am sick at heart.[5]

Barnardo Have you had quiet guard?

Francisco   Not a mouse stirring.   10

1 halt and reveal/disclose/identify★
2 a password? a declaration of loyalty? More likely the latter.
3 attentively, dutifully
4 on time
5 inwardly weary

Barnardo Well, good night.

    If you do meet Horatio and Marcellus,

    The rivals[6] of my watch, bid them make haste.

ENTER HORATIO AND MARCELLUS

Francisco I think I hear them. Stand, ho![7] Who's there?

Horatio Friends to this ground.[8]

15 *Marcellus*   And liegemen[9] to the Dane.[10]

Francisco Give you good night.[11]

Marcellus   O, farewell, honest[12] soldier:

    Who hath relieved you?

Francisco   Barnardo has my place.

    Give you good night.

EXIT FRANCISCO

Marcellus   Holla![13] Barnardo!

Barnardo   Say,[14]

    What, is Horatio there?

---

6 partners, colleagues

7 halt

8 land, region, country

9 faithful subjects / followers

10 kings were spoken of as identical with the countries / regions they ruled: "Norway" = both the king and the country; "Denmark" or "the Dane" = Denmark

11 may God give you a good night (farewell)

12 virtuous, honorable

13 not "hello," but an exclamation of pleasure

14 "say" = the stress of the final iambic foot: GIVE you good NIGHT. / HolLA barNARdo. / SAY. What is *printed* as *three* lines is thus, metrically (prosodically), only one iambic pentameter line. The lines are separated and differently indented in order to indicate (1) the separate speakers and (2) the prosody.

Horatio   A piece of him.

Barnardo Welcome, Horatio. Welcome, good Marcellus.   20

Marcellus What, has this thing appeared again to-night?

Barnardo I have seen nothing.

✱ *Marcellus* Horatio says 'tis but our fantasy,[15]

eyes ⟋ And will not let belief take hold of him

Touching[16] this dreaded sight, twice seen of us;   25

Therefore I have entreated him along

With us, to watch the minutes[17] of this night,

That if again this apparition come,

He may approve[18] our eyes and speak to it.

Horatio   Tush, tush, 'twill not appear.

Barnardo   Sit down awhile;   30

And let us once again assail[19] your ears,

That are so fortified against our story

What we have two nights seen.

Horatio   Well, sit we down,

And let us hear Barnardo speak of this.

Barnardo Last night of all,[20]   35

When yond same star that's westward from the pole[21]

Had made his course t'illume[22] that part of heaven

Where now it burns, Marcellus and myself,

15 fancy, imagination✱
16 concerning, about
17 probably not literally "minutes," but "moments, small stretches of time"
18 confirm, attest to with authority
19 address, attack
20 most of all
21 pole star
22 to light up (the apostrophe is here a metrical convention, indicating that the consonant which it follows is not to be scanned—that is, is not included in the metrical accounting)

The bell then beating one[23] —

ENTER GHOST

40 *Marcellus* Peace,[24] break thee off. Look where it[25] comes again!

Barnardo In the same figure like[26] like the king that's dead.

Marcellus Thou art a scholar;[27] speak to it, Horatio.

Barnardo Looks 'a[28] not like the king? Mark[29] it, Horatio.

Horatio Most like. It harrows[30] me with fear and wonder.

Barnardo It would[31] be spoke to.

45 *Marcellus*   Speak to[32] it, Horatio.

Horatio What art thou that usurp'st this time of night,

Together with that fair[33] and warlike form

In which the majesty of buried Denmark[34]

Did sometimes march?[35] By[36] heaven I charge[37] thee, speak!

Marcellus It is offended.

50 *Barnardo*   See, it stalks[38] away!

Horatio Stay![39] speak, speak! I charge thee, speak!

---

23 public clocks were largely unknown; the hours were generally told ["tolled"] by bells

24 hush, be silent

25 the use of "it" rather than "he" emphasizes the Ghost's non-humanness

26 shape/form

27 a university student, an educated person

28 he★

29 observe, notice★

30 pierces, cuts through (the harrow, set with iron teeth, is attached to a plow)

31 wants to

32 some texts have "question it"

33 pleasing★

34 again, the dead king of Denmark, Hamlet's father, also named Hamlet

35 march, walk

36 in the name of

37 command, exhort★

38 walks proudly

39 stop★

EXIT GHOST

'Tis gone, and will not[40] answer.

Barnardo How now,[41] Horatio! You tremble and look pale.
Is not this something more than fantasy?
What think you on't?[42]   55

Horatio   Before my God, I might not this believe
Without the sensible and true avouch[43]
Of mine own eyes.

Marcellus   Is it not like the king?

Horatio   As thou art to thyself.
Such was the very armor he had on   60
When he the ambitious Norway combated;[44]
So frowned he once, when in an angry parle,[45]
He smote the sledded Polacks[46] on the ice.
'Tis strange.

Marcellus Thus twice before, and jump at this dead[47] hour,   65
With martial stalk hath he gone by our watch.

Horatio   In what particular[48] thought to work[49] I know not;
But in the gross and scope of my opinion,[50]
This bodes some strange eruption to our state.[51]

---

40 does not wish to
41 ah-ha!
42 of it
43 perceptible and truthful confirmation
44 COMbaTED
45 conference with an enemy
46 Polish troops on sledges
47 exactly / precisely at this profoundly quiet, still
48 single / individual / private*
49 accomplish, carry out
50 so far as I am able to understand
51 this indicates / predicts some violent outbreak in our state

¿what does the ghost look like?

70 *Marcellus* Good now,[52] sit down, and tell me, he that knows,[53]
　　　　　Why this same strict and most observant watch[54]
　　　　　So nightly toils the subject[55] of the land,
　　　　　And why such daily cast of brazen[56] cannon,
　　　　　And foreign mart[57] for implements of war,
75　　　Why such impress[58] of shipwrights, whose sore[59] task
　　　　　Does not divide the Sunday from the week[60] —
　　　　　What might be toward[61] that this sweaty[62] haste
　　　　　Doth make the night joint-laborer[63] with the day?
　　　　　Who is't that can inform me?

Horatio　　　　　　　　　　That can I —
80　　　At least, the whisper[64] goes so. Our last king,
　　　　　Whose image even but now appeared to us,
　　　　　Was, as you know, by Fortinbras of Norway
　　　　　Pricked on by a most emulate[65] pride,
　　　　　Dared to the combat, in which our valiant Hamlet —
85　　　For so this side of our known world esteemed[66] him —
　　　　　Did slay this Fortinbras, who, by a sealed compact,[67]

52 good/honored sir, now
53 if you know
54 the same watch that he and his fellows keep every night is being enforced all over Denmark
55 encloses/entangles the subjects/inhabitants
56 casting (as in a foundry) of brass
57 trade
58 conscription, involuntary service
59 laborious, painful
60 Sunday, the traditional day of rest, is for them only another working day
61 coming, approaching, impending
62 laborious
63 co-worker
64 rumor
65 envious, covetous, imitative
66 considered, judged
67 an agreement/covenant/contract attested/certified by a formal wax seal

Well ratified by law and heraldry.[68]
Did forfeit with his life[69] all those his lands
Which he stood seized of,[70] to the conqueror:
Against the which, a moiety competent[71]   90
Was gagèd[72] by our king, which had[73] returned
To the inheritance of Fortinbras,
Had he been vanquisher – as, by the same cov'nant[74]
And carriage of the article designed[75]
His fell to Hamlet. Now, sir, young Fortinbras,   95
Of unimproved mettle[76] hot and full,
Hath in the skirts[77] of Norway here and there
Sharked up[78] a list of lawless resolutes[79]
For food and diet[80] to some enterprise
That hath a stomach in't;[81] which is no other –   100
As it doth well appear unto our state[82] –
But[83] to recover of us, by strong hand
And terms compulsatory, those foresaid lands
So by his father lost. And this, I take it,

68 "heraldry" probably means, here, the traditional practices of knighthood
69 along with his life
70 possessed
71 an equal amount
72 wagered, risked, staked
73 would have
74 agreement, contract
75 and meaning of the intended/planned terms/conditions
76 untried/wild temperament/spirit
77 outskirts, borders
78 collected hastily/indiscriminately
79 a roster of men of determination/desperadoes
80 as the means to provide meat/substance for
81 relish, boldness, courage, bravery ("food and diet" are keyed to "stomach,"
   then regarded as the center of passion and emotion) in it
82 realm, country*
83 except

105 Is the main motive of our preparations,
The source of this our watch and the chief head[84]
Of this post-haste and romage[85] in the land.
Barnardo I think it be no other but e'en[86] so:
Well may it sort[87] that this portentous[88] figure
110 Comes armèd through our watch so like the king
That was and is the question[89] of these wars.
Horatio A mote it is to trouble the mind's eye.[90]
In the most high and palmy[91] state of Rome,
A little ere the mightiest Julius fell,
115 The graves stood tenantless and the sheeted dead[92]
Did squeak and gibber[93] in the Roman streets,
As[94] stars with trains of fire and dews of blood,
Disasters[95] in the sun, and the moist star[96]
Upon whose influence[97] Neptune's empire[98] stands
120 Was sick almost to doomsday with eclipse.[99]

84 source, origin
85 hurry/speed and commotion/bustle
86 even
87 be appropriate
88 ominous, awesome
89 subject
90 Matthew 7.3: "And why beholdest thou the mote that is in thy brother's eye, but considerest not the beam that is in thine own eye?"
91 triumphant, flourishing
92 winding sheets/shrouds were usually white
93 unintelligible/inarticulate speech
94 while
95 unfavorable astrological aspects/positions
96 the moon
97 ethereal fluids were thought to flow from astral bodies, influencing people, things, and events
98 the ocean
99 almost to darkness (Matthew 24.29: on Christ's return "shall the sun be darkened, and the moon shall not give her light")

And even the like precurse[100] of fierce[101] events,
As harbingers preceding still[102] the fates[103]
And prologue to the omen coming on,[104]
Have heaven and earth together demonstrated
Unto our climatures[105] and countrymen.   125

ENTER GHOST

But soft, behold! Lo, where it comes again!
I'll cross it,[106] though it blast[107] me. Stay, illusion![108]

GHOST SPREADS ITS ARMS

If thou hast any sound, or use of voice,
Speak to me.
If there be any good thing to be done,   130
That may to thee do ease and grace to me,
Speak to me.
If thou art privy to thy country's fate,
Which, happily, foreknowing may avoid,
O, speak!   135
Or if thou hast uphoarded in thy life
Extorted[109] treasure in the womb of earth,
For which, they say, you spirits oft walk in death,

---

100 presaging, foreshadowing
101 some texts have "feared"
102 always*
103 the three goddesses controlling human destiny
104 advancing
105 region, climate
106 intersect its path, confront it
107 blight, wither, curse
108 deception, delusion
109 acquired illicitly, by force

THE COCK CROWS

Speak of it. Stay, and speak! Stop it, Marcellus.
140 *Marcellus* Shall I strike at it with my partisan?[110]
Horatio Do, if it will not stand.
Barnardo   'Tis here!
Horatio   'Tis here!

EXIT GHOST

Marcellus 'Tis gone!
We do it wrong, being[111] so majestical,
To offer it the show of violence,[112]
145 For it is, as the air, invulnerable,
And our vain blows malicious mockery.
Barnardo It was about to speak, when the cock crew.
Horatio And then it started like a guilty thing
Upon[113] a fearful summons. I have heard
150 The cock, that is the trumpet to the morn,
Doth with his lofty and shrill-sounding throat
Awake the god of day, and at his warning,
Whether in sea or fire, in earth or air,[114]
The extravagant and erring spirit[115] hies
155 To his confine.[116] And of the truth herein
This present object made probation.[117]

110 long-handled weapon with lateral blade(s)
111 it being
112 VIoLENCE
113 because of, after
114 fire, water, earth, air: then considered the four basic elements
115 straggling, fantastically absurd / excessive and wandering ghost
116 hurries to his place of confinement (usually the grave)
117 proof

Marcellus It faded on the crowing of the cock.
  Some say that ever 'gainst[118] that season comes
  Wherein our Saviour's birth is celebrated,
  The bird of dawning singeth all night long,   160
  And then, they say, no spirit dares stir abroad,
  The nights are wholesome, then, no planets strike,[119]
  No fairy takes,[120] nor witch hath power to charm,[121]
  So hallowed and so gracious[122] is the time.
Horatio So have I heard and do in part believe it.   165
  But, look, the morn, in russet[123] mantle clad,
  Walks o'er the dew of[124] yon high eastward hill.
  Break we our watch up;[125] and by my advice,
  Let us impart what we have seen to-night
  Unto young Hamlet; for, upon my life,   170
  This spirit, dumb to us, will speak to him.
  Do you consent we shall acquaint him with it,
  As needful in our loves, fitting our duty?
Marcellus Let's do't, I pray; and I this morning know
  Where we shall find him most convenient.[126]   175

EXEUNT

118 always near/in anticipation of
119 smite (as with a weapon), afflict, attack, wound, kill
120 bewitches
121 enchant
122 holy/sanctified and full of grace
123 reddish/yellowish brown
124 on (dew was thought to fall from the heavens)
125 let us stop, interrupt our watch
126 conveniently

SCENE 2
The castle

ENTER CLAUDIUS (KING OF DENMARK), GERTRUDE
(THE QUEEN), HAMLET (SON OF THE QUEEN AND THE
RECENTLY DECEASED KING, ALSO NAMED HAMLET),
POLONIUS (COUNCILLOR OF STATE), LAERTES
(POLONIUS'S SON), CORNELIUS AND VOLTEMAND
(AMBASSADORIAL MESSENGERS), AND OTHERS

Claudius Though yet of Hamlet our dear brother's death
 The memory be green, and that it us befitted[1]
 To bear our hearts in grief and our whole kingdom
 To be contracted[2] in one brow of woe,
5 Yet so far hath discretion fought with nature
 That we with wisest sorrow think on him,
 Together with remembrance of ourselves.
 Therefore our sometime[3] sister, now our queen,
 The imperial jointress[4] to this warlike state,
10 Have we, as 'twere with a defeated[5] joy,
 With an auspicious and a dropping[6] eye,
 With mirth in funeral and with dirge in marriage,
 In equal scale weighing delight and dole,[7]
 Taken to wife. Nor have we herein barred

1 was proper/appropriate
2 narrowed, shrunken
3 previously, formerly
4 legal heir of property (not power) settled on her, upon her marriage to her
 late royal husband
5 spoiled, defaced, disfigured
6 a propitious/favored by fortune and a depressed/sunken
7 sorrow, grief, mourning

Your better wisdoms, which have freely gone   15
With this affair along. For all, our thanks.
Now follows that you know young Fortinbras,
Holding a weak supposal of our worth,[8]
Or thinking by our late dear brother's death
Our state to be disjoint and out of frame,[9]   20
Colleagued[10] with this dream of his advantage,[11]
He hath not failed to pester us with message
Importing[12] the surrender of those lands
Lost by his father, with all bonds[13] of law,
To our most valiant brother. So much for him.   25
Now for ourself and for this time of meeting.
Thus much the business is: we have here writ
To Norway, uncle of young Fortinbras, –
Who, impotent[14] and bed-rid, scarcely hears
Of this his nephew's purpose,   to suppress   30
His further gait[15] herein, in that the levies,[16]
The lists and full proportions,[17] are all made
Out of his subject:[18] And we here dispatch
You, good Cornelius, and you, Voltimand,
For bearers of this greeting to old Norway;   35

8 a weak opinion of our (my) character/qualities
9 coming apart and out of order
10 joined (colLEAGUed)
11 superiority, superior position
12 with messages (or messengers/envoys) carrying/conveying
13 according to all agreements, covenants, contracts
14 decrepit, weak
15 Fortinbras's further movement
16 because the enlistments
17 the rolls and (their) abundant/copious size/numbers
18 Norway's subjects

Giving to you no further personal power
To business with the king, more than the scope
Of these delated articles[19] allow.
Farewell, and let your haste commend your duty.

40 *Cornelius, Voltimand* In that and all things will we show our duty.
   Claudius   We doubt it nothing. Heartily farewell.

EXEUNT VOLTIMAND AND CORNELIUS

And now, Laertes, what's the news with you?
You told us of some suit.[20] What is't, Laertes?
You cannot speak of reason to the Dane[21]
45 And lose your voice.[22] What wouldst thou beg, Laertes,
That shall not be my offer, not thy asking?[23]
The head is not more native[24] to the heart,
The hand more instrumental[25] to the mouth,
Than is the throne of Denmark to thy father.
What wouldst thou have, Laertes?

50 *Laertes*   My dread[26] lord,
Your leave and favor[27] to return to France,[28]
From whence though willingly I came to Denmark
To show my duty in your coronation,

19 expanded/explanatory writings/documents
20 petition, request
21 Claudius himself
22 waste your breath
23 that would not be given to Laertes by the King, without Laertes having to
   ask
24 naturally connected, closely related
25 useful, of service
26 revered★
27 permission and indulgence
28 guests customarily required an aristocratic host's permission to leave

Yet now, I must confess, that duty done,
My thoughts and wishes bend again toward France   55
And bow them to your gracious leave and pardon.[29]

Claudius Have you your father's leave? What says Polonius?

Polonius He hath, my lord, wrung from me my slow[30] leave
By laborsome petition,[31] and at last
Upon his will I sealed my hard[32] consent.   60
I do beseech you, give him leave to go.

Claudius Take thy fair[33] hour, Laertes, Time be thine,
And thy best graces[34] spend it at thy will!
But now, my cousin Hamlet, and my son — [35]

Hamlet (*aside*) A little more than kin, and less than kind.[36]   65

Claudius How is it that the clouds[37] still hang on you?

Hamlet Not so, my lord. I am too much i' the sun.[38]

Gertrude Good Hamlet, cast thy nighted color[39] off,
And let thine eye look like a friend on Denmark.
Do not for ever with thy vailèd[40] lids   70
Seek for thy noble father in the dust.

29 permission, indulgence
30 reluctant
31 entreaty, supplication
32 upon his desire I granted (figuratively, "set my seal upon") my difficult-to-
   give
33 advantageous, favorable
34 luck
35 cousin: used freely for relatives less close than a brother or sister; son: a son by
   marriage was termed a son, just as a daughter by marriage was termed a
   daughter*
36 kin: relative; kind: kindly, showing goodwill (*and* having the same nature)
37 darkness, gloom
38 the light of royal attention (*and* in the position of "son")
39 dark appearance
40 lowered, cast down

Thou know'st 'tis common; all that lives must die,
Passing through nature to eternity.[41]

Hamlet   Ay, madam, it is common.[42]

Gertrude   If it be,

75   Why seems it so particular with[43] thee?

Hamlet   Seems, madam! nay it is; I know not "seems."
'Tis not alone my inky[44] cloak, good mother,
Nor customary suits[45] of solemn black,
Nor windy suspiration of forced[46] breath,

80   No, nor the fruitful[47] river in the eye,
Nor the dejected havior[48] of the visage,
Together with all forms, moods, shapes of grief,
That can denote[49] me truly. These indeed seem,
For they are actions that a man might play,[50]

85   But I have that within which passeth[51] show;
These but the trappings and the suits of woe.

Claudius   'Tis sweet and commendable in your nature, Hamlet,
To give these mourning duties to your father,
But you must know your father lost a father,

90   That father lost, lost his, and the survivor bound
In filial obligation for some term

41 iyTERniTIE/
42 universal (*and* vulgar)
43 personal/peculiar to
44 black (the color of mourning)
45 clothing
46 sighing of artificial/laborious/constrained
47 copious, abundant
48 bearing, deportment
49 describe, distinguish
50 act the part of, trifle/sport with
51 exceeds, surpasses★

To do obsequious[52] sorrow: But to persever
In obstinate condolement is a course[53]
Of impious stubbornness. 'Tis unmanly grief,
It shows a will most incorrect[54] to heaven,   95
A heart unfortified, a mind impatient,
An understanding simple and unschooled.[55]
For what we know must be, and is, as common
As any the most vulgar thing to sense,[56]
Why should we in our peevish opposition   100
Take it to heart? Fie, 'tis a fault to heaven,
A fault against the dead, a fault to nature,
To reason most absurd, whose common theme
Is death of fathers, and who still hath cried,
From the first corse[57] till he that died to-day,   105
"This must be so." We pray you, throw to earth
This unprevailing[58] woe, and think of us
As of a father, for let the world take note
You are the most immediate[59] to our throne,
And with no less nobility of love   110
Than that which dearest father bears his son
Do I impart[60] toward you. For your intent
In going back to school in Wittenberg,

---

52 obsequious: that which is appropriate for funerals (obsequy: funeral rites)
53 lamentation / grieving is a way of acting
54 uncorrected, unchastened
55 feeble / weak and undisciplined
56 common / ordinary to the senses
57 corpse*
58 ineffectual, useless
59 direct successor
60 make this known, relate, tell

It is most retrograde[61] to our desire,
115　And we beseech you: bend you[62] to remain
Here, in the cheer and comfort of our eye,
Our chiefest courtier, cousin, and our son.
Gertrude　Let not thy mother lose[63] her prayers, Hamlet.
I pray thee, stay with us, go not to Wittenberg.
120　*Hamlet*　I shall in all my best[64] obey you, madam.
Claudius　Why, 'tis a loving and a fair reply:
Be as ourself in Denmark. Madam, come.
This gentle[65] and unforced accord of Hamlet
Sits smiling to my heart, in grace[66] whereof
125　No jocund health[67] that Denmark drinks to-day,
But the great cannon to the clouds shall tell,
And the king's rouse[68] the heavens shall bruit[69] again,
Re-speaking earthly thunder. Come away.

TRUMPETS. EXEUNT ALL BUT HAMLET

Hamlet　O, that this too too solid[70] flesh would melt,
130　Thaw and resolve[71] itself into a dew!
Or that the Everlasting had not fixed
His canon[72] 'gainst self-slaughter! O God, God,

61　contrary, repugnant, opposed
62　turn your mind
63　waste, forfeit
64　as best I can
65　gentlemanly, well-bred★
66　thanks, thanksgiving
67　cheerful toast
68　full draught/bumper of liquor
69　clamor, create a din, make a great noise
70　some texts have "sullied"
71　dissolve
72　rule, law

How weary, stale, flat and unprofitable
Seem to me all the uses[73] of this world!
Fie on't, ah fie, 'tis an unweeded garden   135
That grows to seed: things rank and gross in nature[74]
Possess it merely.[75] That it should come to this –
But two months dead – nay, not so much, not two –
So excellent a king,[76] that was to this[77]
Hyperion to a satyr,[78] so loving to my mother   140
That he might not beteem[79] the winds of heaven
Visit[80] her face too roughly. Heaven and earth!
Must I remember? Why, she would hang on him
As if increase of appetite[81] had grown
By what it fed on – and yet, within a month –   145
Let me not think on't: frailty, thy name is woman!
A little month, or ere[82] those shoes were old
With which she followed my poor father's body
Like Niobe,[83] all tears – why she, even she –
O God, a beast that wants discourse[84] of reason   150
Would have mourned longer   married with my uncle,

73 habits, practices, customs
74 of nature / character
75 absolutely, altogether, unconditionally
76 Hamlet's father
77 Hamlet's uncle
78 the Sun God compared to a wood demon (half beast, half human)
79 allow, think fit / proper
80 come to, afflict
81 desire, craving
82 before*
83 mother of six sons and six daughters, who taunted the gods because of her fertility; they responded by killing all her children; Niobe was turned to stone but went on weeping
84 lacks the faculty / power

My father's brother, but no more like my father
Than I to Hercules. Within a month,
Ere yet the salt of most unrighteous[85] tears
155 Had left the flushing in her gallèd eyes,[86]
She married. O, most wicked speed, to post
With such dexterity[87] to incestuous[88] sheets!
It is not nor it cannot come to good.
But break, my heart; for I must hold my tongue.

ENTER HORATIO, MARCELLUS, AND BARNARDO

Horatio   Hail to your lordship!
160 *Hamlet*   I am glad to see you well.
Horatio! Or I do forget myself.[89]
Horatio   The same, my lord, and your poor servant ever.
Hamlet   Sir, my good friend; I'll change that name[90] with you:
And what make you from Wittenberg,[91] Horatio? (*turning*)
165 Marcellus.[92]
Marcellus My good lord.
Hamlet   I am very glad to see you.[93] Good even, sir.[94]
But what, in faith, make you from Wittenberg?

85 wicked
86 stopped creating the rushing of blood to her sore / irriated eyes
87 to hurry with such facility
88 Leviticus 20.21: "And if a man shall take his brother's wife, it is an unclean thing"
89 unless I have forgotten myself / who I am
90 exchange the name of "servant" with you: to put oneself in the role of a "servant" was an expression of good manners, a form of greeting or leave-taking
91 what are you doing away from Wittenberg?
92 an acknowledgment of recognition and a greeting
93 spoken to Marcellus
94 spoken to Barnardo? or to Marcellus? or both?

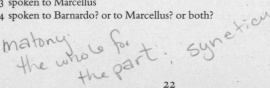
matony.
the whole for
the part. synetica

Horatio   A truant disposition,[95] good my lord.

Hamlet   I would not hear[96] your enemy say so,   170
Nor shall you do mine ear that violence,
To make it truster[97] of your own report
Against yourself. I know you are no truant.
But what is your affair[98] in Elsinore?
We'll teach you to drink deep ere you depart.[99]   175

Horatio My lord, I came to see your father's funeral.

Hamlet I pray thee, do not mock me, fellow-student.
I think it was to see my mother's wedding.

Horatio Indeed, my lord, it followed hard upon.

Hamlet Thrift, thrift, Horatio! The funeral baked meats[100]   180
Did coldly furnish forth[101] the marriage tables.
Would I had met my dearest foe in heaven[102]
Or[103] ever I had seen that day, Horatio!
My father! Methinks[104] I see my father.

Horatio Where, my lord?

Hamlet   In my mind's eye, Horatio.   185

Horatio I saw him once. 'A was a goodly[105] king.

Hamlet 'A was a man, take him for all in all,

---

95 a lazy/loitering nature/mood
96 listen to
97 believer, reliant on
98 business★
99 a negative comment on the King's "deep drinking"
100 meat pies
101 with cold feeling/cold temperatures supply/provide for
102 meeting a "dearest foe" in heaven would mean he is not in hell, where one
    wishes him to be
103 "or," here = "ere," before
104 I think, it seems to me★
105 gracious, courteous, kindly

    I shall not look upon his like again.

    Horatio My lord, I think I saw him yesternight.

190 *Hamlet* Saw? Who?

    Horatio My lord, the King your father.

    Hamlet   The King my father!

    Horatio Season your admiration[106] for awhile

    With an attent[107] ear, till I may deliver,[108]

    Upon the witness of these gentlemen,

    This marvel to you.

195 *Hamlet*   For God's love, let me hear.

    Horatio Two nights together[109] had these gentlemen,

    Marcellus and Barnardo, on their watch

    In the dead vast and middle of the night,

    Been thus encountered. A figure like your father,

200   Armèd at point[110] exactly, cap-a-pe,[111]

    Appears before them, and with solemn march[112]

    Goes slow and stately by them. Thrice he walked

    By their oppressed[113] and fear-surprisèd eyes,

    Within his truncheon's length,[114] whilst they, distilled

205   Almost to jelly with the act[115] of fear,

    Stand dumb and speak not to him. This to me

    In dreadful[116] secrecy impart they did,

106 moderate your wonder
107 attentive
108 set forth, describe
109 consecutively
110 at the ready
111 head to toe
112 step, movement
113 startled, overwhelmed
114 in the space of a spear-shaft
115 melted / dissolved by the operation
116 fearful, reverential

And I with them the third night kept the watch,
Where, as they had delivered – both in time,
Form of the thing, each word made true and good –   210
The apparition comes. I knew[117] your father:
These hands[118] are not more like.

Hamlet   But where was this?

Marcellus My lord, upon the platform where we watched.

Hamlet   Did you not speak to it?

Horatio   My lord, I did,
But answer made it none. Yet once methought   215
It lifted up its head and did address[119]
Itself to motion, like as it would speak,
But even[120] then the morning cock crew loud,
And at the sound it shrunk in haste away,
And vanished from our sight.

Hamlet   'Tis very strange.   220

Horatio   As I do live, my honored lord, 'tis true,
And we did think it writ down in our duty[121]
To let you know of it.

Hamlet   Indeed, indeed, sirs. But this troubles me.
Hold[122] you the watch to-night?

All   We do, my lord.   225

Hamlet   Armed, say you?

All   Armed, my lord.

Hamlet   From top to toe?

---

117 recognized
118 his own, held out in front of him
119 commit, turn
120 just
121 part of our office/responsibility
122 keep

ACT I • SCENE 2

All   My lord, from head to foot.

Hamlet Then saw you not his face?

230 *Horatio* O, yes, my lord. He wore his beaver[123] up.

Hamlet What, looked he frowningly?

Horatio A countenance more in sorrow than in anger.

Hamlet Pale or red?

Horatio Nay, very pale.

Hamlet   And fixed his eyes upon you?

Horatio Most constantly.

235 *Hamlet*   I would I had been there.

Horatio It would have much amazed you.

Hamlet Very like, very like. Stayed it long?

Horatio While one with moderate haste might tell[124] a hundred.

Marcellus, Barnardo Longer, longer.

Horatio Not when I saw't.

240 *Hamlet*   His beard was grizzled, no?

Horatio   It was, as I have seen it in his life,
A sable silvered.[125]

Hamlet   I will watch to-night;
Perchance 'twill walk again.

Horatio   I warrant[126] it will.

Hamlet If it assume my noble father's person,

245 I'll speak to it, though hell itself should gape
And bid me hold my peace. I pray you all,
If you have hitherto concealed this sight,
Let it be tenable[127] in your silence still,

---

123 bottom of a helmet's face-guard
124 count
125 a silvered sable
126 guarantee, promise
127 kept, held

And whatsoever else shall hap[128] to-night,
Give it an understanding, but no tongue: 250
I will requite your loves. So, fare you well.
Upon the platform, 'twixt eleven and twelve,
I'll visit you.
All   Our duty[129] to your honour.
Hamlet Your loves,[130] as mine to you. Farewell.

EXEUNT ALL BUT HAMLET

My father's spirit – in arms! All is not well.   255
I doubt[131] some foul play. Would the night were come!
Till then sit still, my soul. Foul deeds will rise,
Though all the earth o'erwhelm[132] them, to men's eyes.

EXIT

128 chance to happen
129 respect (a formulaic greeting or farewell)
130 Hamlet rejects the formula. He wishes more than "duty": as he has already
     said, he wants to have their "love," meaning affectionate rather than
     obligatory loyalty
131 fear, suspect*
132 cover, bury

SCENE 3
A room

ENTER LAERTES AND OPHELIA

Laertes   My necessaries are embarked. Farewell.
    And, sister, as the winds give benefit[1]
    And convoy is assistant,[2] do not sleep,
    But let me hear from you.
Ophelia   Do you doubt that?
5   *Laertes*   For[3] Hamlet and the trifling of his favor,[4]
    Hold it a fashion and a toy in blood,[5]
    A violet in the youth of primy nature,[6]
    Forward,[7] not permanent, sweet, not lasting,
    The perfume and suppliance[8] of a minute.
    No more.
Ophelia   No more but so?
10 *Laertes*   Think it no more.
    For nature crescent does not grow alone[9]
    In thews and bulk,[10] but, as this temple waxes,[11]
    The inward service[12] of the mind and soul

1 when the winds are favorable
2 means of transportation are available
3 as for
4 dallying of his attention
5 a pretense and fooling about of disposition/mood (modern usage: "of young hormones")
6 a flowering of a young man in his prime
7 precocious, ahead of its time
8 diversion, pastime
9 for growing nature does not grow only
10 bodily strength/muscles and size
11 this body grows★
12 performance, duties

Grows wide withal.[13] Perhaps he loves you now,
And now no soil nor cautel[14] doth besmirch[15]   15
The virtue of his will.[16] But you must fear:
His greatness weighed,[17] his will is not his own,
For he himself is subject to his birth.
He may not, as unvalued persons[18] do,
Carve[19] for himself, for on his choice depends   20
The safety and health of this whole state,
And therefore must his choice be circumscribed
Unto the voice and yielding of that body[20]
Whereof he is the head. Then if he says he loves you,
It fits your wisdom so far to believe it   25
As he in his particular act and place
May give his saying deed,[21] which is no further
Than the main voice[22] of Denmark goes withal.[23]
Then weigh what loss your honor may sustain,
If with too credent ear you list[24] his songs,   30
Or lose your heart, or your chaste treasure open
To his unmastered importunity.[25]
Fear it, Ophelia, fear it, my dear sister,

13 increased in range / extent along with the rest
14 moral stain / tarnish nor trickery / craftiness
15 discolor, dim the luster of
16 desire
17 his high rank considered
18 people not of high rank
19 take his pleasure
20 consent of that body (the state)
21 may transform his words into actions
22 principal voice (the King)
23 goes along with
24 trusting ear you listen to
25 untamed relentless urging

And keep you in the rear of[26] your affection;
35   Out of the shot[27] and danger of desire.
The chariest[28] maid is prodigal enough,
If she unmask[29] her beauty to the moon.
Virtue itself 'scapes not calumnious strokes.[30]
The canker galls[31] the infants of the spring
40   Too oft before their buttons be disclosed,[32]
And in the morn and liquid dew of youth
Contagious blastments are most imminent.[33]
Be wary, then; best safety lies in fear.
Youth to itself rebels, though none else near.
45 *Ophelia*   I shall the effect[34] of this good lesson keep,
As watchman to my heart. But, good my brother,
Do not, as some ungracious[35] pastors do,
Show me the steep and thorny way to heaven,
Whiles, like a puffed[36] and reckless libertine,
50   Himself the primrose path of dalliance treads,
And recks not his own rede.[37]

ENTER POLONIUS

Laertes   O, fear me not.

26 in the back ranks (a military reference continued in the next line)
27 shooting
28 most cautious
29 uncover, reveal
30 slanderous blows
31 the rotting disease injures
32 their buds are opened
33 diseases are most threatening
34 meaning, drift, tenor
35 unattractive, graceless, discourteous
36 vain, inflated
37 pays no attention to his own advice

I stay too long. But here my father comes.
A double blessing is a double grace:[38]
Occasion smiles upon a second leave.[39]

Polonius Yet here, Laertes? Aboard, aboard, for shame!   55
The wind sits in the shoulder of your sail,
And you are stayed for.[40] There — my blessing with thee,
And these few precepts in thy memory
Look thou character.[41] Give thy thoughts no tongue,
Nor any unproportioned thought his act.[42]   60
Be thou familiar, but by no means vulgar.[43]
Those friends thou hast, and their adoption tried,[44]
Grapple[45] them to thy soul with hoops of steel,
But do not dull thy palm[46] with entertainment[47]
Of each new-hatched, unfledged courage.[48] Beware   65
Of entrance to a quarrel, but being in
Bear't[49] that the opposèd may beware of thee.
Give every man thy ear, but few thy voice;
Take each man's censure, but reserve thy judgment
Costly thy habit[50] as thy purse can buy,   70

38 having had his father's blessing, he is about to have it again
39 circumstances smile upon a second leave-taking
40 waited for
41 be attentive / careful that you engrave / write
42 disproportionate / out-of-balance thought its action / deed
43 affable / courteous, but never coarse / lacking in good taste
44 association with you tested
45 grasp, take hold of
46 but do not blunt / tarnish your grip / success
47 receiving, accommodating
48 callow / crude / undeveloped person
49 carry / acquit yourself
50 clothing, dress★

But not expressed in fancy[51] – rich, not gaudy;
For the apparel oft proclaims the man,
And they in France of the best rank and station
Are of a most select and generous chief[52] in that.
75 Neither a borrower nor a lender be,
For loan oft loses both itself and friend,
And borrowing dulls the edge of husbandry.[53]
This above all: to thine own self be true,
And it must follow, as the night the day,
80 Thou canst not then be false to any man.
Farewell: my blessing season[54] this in thee!
Laertes Most humbly do I take my leave, my lord.
Polonius The time invites you. Go, your servants tend.[55]
Laertes Farewell, Ophelia; and remember well
What I have said to you.
85 Ophelia   'Tis in my memory locked,
And you yourself shall keep the key of it.
Laertes Farewell.

EXIT LAERTES

Polonius What is't, Ophelia, be hath said to you?
Ophelia So please you, something touching[56] the Lord Hamlet.
90 Polonius Marry,[57] well bethought.[58]

---

51 whims, caprices
52 a most excellent and gallant/noble chief position
53 thrift*
54 ripen, mature
55 await you
56 relating to, concerning*
57 an exclamation (originally an oath employing the Virgin Mary's name)*
58 considered

'Tis told me, he hath very oft of late
Given private time to you, and you yourself
Have of your audience been most free and bounteous.[59]
If it be so, as so 'tis put on[60] me,
And that in way of caution, I must tell you   95
You do not understand yourself so clearly
As it behooves[61] my daughter and your honor.
What is between you? Give me up the truth.
Ophelia He hath, my lord, of late made many tenders[62]
Of his affection to me.   100
Polonius Affection! pooh! you speak like a green girl,
Unsifted[63] in such perilous circumstance.
Do you believe his tenders, as you call them?
Ophelia I do not know, my lord, what I should think.
Polonius Marry, I will teach you. Think yourself a baby   105
That you have ta'en[64] these tenders for true pay,[65]
Which are not sterling.[66] Tender yourself more dearly;[67]
Or   not to crack the wind of the poor phrase,
Running it[68] thus – you'll tender me a fool.[69]

59 of your reception of visits been most generous and liberal
60 told to, confided in
61 befits, is appropriate for
62 offers
63 inexperienced
64 taken
65 payment (Polonius is punning on commercial "tenders"; in commerce
    "payment" = "satisfaction")
66 (1) English currency (as in "pound sterling"); (2) pure, excellent
67 (1) worth more, as a person; (2) worth more, more costly, in commercial
    terms
68 one "cracks the wind" of a horse by "running it" too hard: Polonius not only
    puns incessantly, but comments on himself punning
69 (1) a fool (Ophelia herself); (2) a baby

110 *Ophelia* My lord, he hath importuned me with love
　　　In honorable fashion.[70]

　　Polonius Ay, fashion you may call it. Go to, go to.[71]

　　Ophelia And hath given countenance[72] to his speech, my lord,
　　　With almost all the holy vows of heaven.

115 *Polonius* Ay, springes to catch woodcocks.[73] I do know,
　　　When the blood burns, how prodigal[74] the soul
　　　Lends the tongue vow.[75] These blazes, daughter,
　　　Giving more light than heat, extinct[76] in both,
　　　Even in their promise, as it is a-making,

120 　You must not take for fire. From this time
　　　Be something scanter of your maiden presence.[77]
　　　Set your entreatments[78] at a higher rate
　　　Than a command to parley.[79] For[80] Lord Hamlet,
　　　Believe so much in him, that he is young

125 　And with a larger tether[81] may he walk
　　　Than may be given you. In few,[82] Ophelia,
　　　Do not believe his vows, for they are brokers,[83]

70 (1) manner; (2) making, shaping, forming
71 you can't be serious!
72 moral support
73 snares, traps to catch (1) foolish birds, (2) fools
74 lavishly, recklessly
75 the emotions / passions bestow on the tongue solemn promises
76 extinguished
77 more restricted of your virginal presence
78 (1) conversations; (2) negotiations
79 hold discussions, as for a truce or treaty
80 as for
81 the rope / cord with which an animal is tied
82 in a few words, in short
83 middlemen, pimps

Not of that dye[84] which their investments[85] show,
But mere implorators of unholy suits,[86]
Breathing like sanctified and pious bawds,[87]   130
The better to beguile. This is for all:[88]
I would not, in plain terms, from this time forth,
Have you so slander any moment leisure,[89]
As to give words or talk with the Lord Hamlet.
Look to't, I charge you.[90] Come[91] your ways.   135
Ophelia   I shall obey, my lord.

EXEUNT

84 color, nature
85 (1) clothing; (2) money or capital put into a business
86 entreators of unholy causes
87 speaking like sanctified and pious pimps/brothel keepers
88 in sum, finally, once and for all
89 disgrace any moment of leisure
90 attend to it, I command you
91 recover, change

SCENE 4

The castle in Elsinore—a guard platform

ENTER HAMLET, HORATIO, AND MARCELLUS

Hamlet	The air bites shrewdly;[1] it is very cold.
Horatio	It is a nipping and an eager[2] air.
Hamlet	What hour now?
Horatio	I think it lacks of twelve.
Marcellus	No, it is struck.

5   *Horatio*   Indeed? I heard it not. It then draws near the season[3]
   Wherein the spirit held his wont to walk.[4]

A FLOURISH OF TRUMPETS, AND TWO PIECES
(OF ORDNANCE) GO OFF

   What does this mean, my lord?
Hamlet   The king doth wake to-night and takes his rouse,[5]
   Keeps wassail and the swagg'ring up-spring reels,[6]
10   And as he drains his draughts of Rhenish[7] down,
   The kettle-drum and trumpet thus bray out
   The triumph of his pledge.[8]
Horatio   Is it a custom?
Hamlet   Ay, marry, is't,
   But to my mind, though I am native here

---

1 fiercely, wickedly
2 sharp and a keen
3 time
4 made it his habit/custom to walk
5 is awake tonight and is having his drinking bout
6 observes/celebrates sitting and drinking and the showy, leaping, lively dances
7 Rhenish wine
8 toast, drinking to someone's health

And to the manner[9] born, it is a custom   15
More honored in the breach[10] than the observance.
This heavy-headed revel east and west
Makes us traduced and taxed of[11] other nations.
They clepe[12] us drunkards, and with swinish[13] phrase
Soil our addition,[14] and indeed it takes   20
From[15] our achievements, though performed at height,[16]
The pith and marrow of our attribute.[17]
So oft it chances in particular men
That for some vicious mole of nature[18] in them,
As[19] in their birth, wherein they are not guilty,   25
(Since nature cannot choose his[20] origin)
By the o'ergrowth of some complexion,[21]
Oft breaking down the pales and forts[22] of reason,
Or by some habit that too much o'er-leavens[23]
The form of plausive manners that[24] these men —   30
Carrying, I say, the stamp of one defect,

9 custom, usage
10 breaking
11 maligned/slandered by
12 call
13 gross, coarse
14 name
15 injures
16 though carried out at the highest level
17 the essence and vital part of our reputation
18 defective/debased fault/blemish of character/disposition
19 as if
20 its
21 habit of body or mind (comPLEXiON)
22 fences/boundaries and fortified positions
23 permeates, ferments, corrupts
24 the form of behavior that can be approved of, so that

Being nature's livery or fortune's star,[25]
Their virtues else,[26] be they as pure as grace,
As infinite as man may undergo[27] —
35 Shall in the general[28] censure take corruption
From that particular fault. The dram[29] of evil
Doth all the noble substance often doubt,[30]
To his own scandal.[31]

Horatio   Look, my lord, it comes!

ENTER GHOST

Hamlet Angels and ministers[32] of grace defend us!
40 Be thou a spirit of health,[33] or goblin damned,   → confused
Bring with thee airs from heaven or blasts from hell,   by who the
Be thy intents wicked or charitable,[34]   spirit is
Thou com'st in such a questionable[35] shape
That I will speak to thee. I'll call thee Hamlet,
45 King, father, royal Dane. O, answer me!
Let me not burst in ignorance, but tell
Why thy canonized bones, hearsed[36] in death,
Have burst their cerements,[37] why the sepulcher

25 badge / outerwear, *or* controlling astrological influence
26 otherwise
27 enjoy, partake of
28 overall
29 small quantity
30 the noble essence call into question
31 to its own discredit, disgrace
32 servants
33 goodness
34 loving God and man
35 capable of being asked questions (QUEStionABle)
36 thy consecrated bones, coffined
37 waxed wrappings / shrouds

Wherein we saw thee quietly inurned[38]
Hath oped his ponderous and marble jaws,   50
To cast thee up again. What may this mean,
That thou, dead corse, again in cómplete steel,[39]
Revisits thus the glimpses of the moon,[40]
Making night hideous and we fools of nature[41]
So horridly to shake our disposition[42]   55
With thoughts beyond the reaches of our souls?
need ← Say, why is this? Wherefore? What should we do?
of understanding

GHOST BECKONS HAMLET

Horatio   It beckons you to go away with it,
As if it some impartment[43] did desire
To you alone.
Marcellus   Look, with what courteous action[44]   60
It waves you to a more removèd ground.[45]
But do not go with it.
Horatio   No, by no means.
Hamlet   It will not speak. Then I will follow it.
Horatio   Do not, my lord.
Hamlet   Why, what should be the fear?
I do not set my life at a pin's fee,[46]   65

38 motionlessly entombed
39 a full suit of armor
40 the transient/flickering traces/flashes of the moon
41 making night dreadful and we playthings/toys of nature
42 that we shake our constitutions
43 communication
44 gesture
45 distant/secluded place
46 cost, price

And for my soul, what can it do to that,
Being a thing immortal as itself?
It waves me forth again. I'll follow it.

Horatio   What if it tempt you toward the flood,[47] my lord,
70   Or to the dreadful summit of the cliff
That beetles o'er his base[48] into the sea,
And there assume some other horrible form,
Which might deprive your sovereignty of[49] reason
And draw you into madness? Think of it.
75   The very place puts toys of desperation,[50]
Without more motive,[51] into every brain
That looks so many fathoms to the sea
And hears it roar beneath.

Hamlet   It waves me still.
    (*to* Ghost)
Go on; I'll follow thee.

Marcellus   You shall not go, my lord.

80   *Hamlet*   Hold off your hands.

Horatio   Be ruled.[52] You shall not go.

Hamlet   My fate cries out
And makes each petty artere[53] in this body
As hardy[54] as the Nemean lion's nerve.[55]

Irony because the lion was slain by hercules whom Hamlet said he was nothing like before

47 sea
48 scowls over its bottom/foundation
49 your control over
50 tricks/fantastic notions of despair/recklessness
51 without more cause
52 guided, restrained
53 sinew, muscle (ARtere)
54 bold, vigorous
55 muscles/strength of the [magically invulnerable] lion killed by Hercules

Still am I called. Unhand me, gentlemen.
By heaven, I'll make a ghost of him that lets me![56]   85
I say, away!
(*to Ghost*)
      Go on. I'll follow thee.

EXEUNT GHOST AND HAMLET

Horatio	He waxes desperate with imagination.[57]
Marcellus	Let's follow. 'Tis not fit thus to obey him.
Horatio	Have after.[58] To what issue[59] will this come?
Marcellus	Something is rotten in the state of Denmark. 90
Horatio	Heaven will direct[60] it.
Marcellus	Nay, let's follow him.

EXEUNT

56 stops me
57 fancy, fantasy
58 let's go after him
59 outcome, result
60 guide, regulate, straighten out

SCENE 5

On the upper walls of the castle

ENTER GHOST AND HAMLET

Hamlet Whither wilt thou lead me? Speak. I'll go no further.

Ghost Mark me.

Hamlet I will.

Ghost My hour is almost come,
When I to sulf'rous and tormenting flames
Must render up myself.

Hamlet Alas, poor ghost!

5 *Ghost* Pity me not, but lend thy serious hearing
To what I shall unfold.

Hamlet Speak; I am bound[1] to hear.

Ghost So art thou to revenge, when thou shalt hear.

Hamlet What?[2]

Ghost I am thy father's spirit,

10 Doomed for a certain term[3] to walk the night,
And for the day confined to fast[4] in fires,
Till the foul crimes done in my days of nature[5]
Are burnt and purged away. But that I am forbid
To tell the secrets of my prison-house,

15 I could a tale unfold whose lightest[6] word
Would harrow[7] up thy soul, freeze thy young blood,

---

1 duty bound
2 revenge what?
3 condemned/sentenced for a fixed period
4 "Flesh triumphed in the wicked on earth, and hell is of the flesh, though the spirit also be agonized" (H. O. Taylor, *The Mediaeval Mind,* 1:471)
5 sins committed in my earthly life
6 slightest
7 cut through, pierce, lacerate

Make thy two eyes, like stars, start[8] from their spheres,[9]
Thy knotted and combinèd[10] locks to part[11]
And each particular hair to stand on end,
Like quills upon the fretful porpentine.[12]   20
But this eternal blazon must not be[13]
To ears of flesh and blood. List, list, O, list!
If thou didst ever thy dear father love –

Hamlet O God!

Ghost Revenge his foul and most unnatural murder.   *Scenic over-*   25
                                                          look

Hamlet Murder!

Ghost Murder most foul, as in the best it is,
But this most foul, strange and unnatural.   *brother*

Hamlet Haste me to know't, that I, with wings as swift

med. As meditation[14] or the thoughts of love,   30
is not
quick May sweep to my revenge.

Ghost   I find thee apt,
And duller[15] shouldst thou be than the fat weed
                                              claudius
claudius That roots itself in ease on Lethe wharf,[16]
is rooting
himself Wouldst thou not stir[17] in this. Now, Hamlet, hear.
into the 'Tis given out that, sleeping in my orchard,[18] *Garden of*   35
kings spot. A serpent stung me. So the whole ear of Denmark *Eden*

 8 leap, burst
 9 in Ptolemaic astronomy, the stars are planets and exist inside hollow spheres
10 interconnected and joined
11 separate, divide
12 irritable/peevish porcupine
13 eternal description must not be given to/heard by
14 thought
15 more listless/lethargic
16 bank of the River Lethe (in Hades: one sip and the drinker's entire past is
   forgotten)
17 if you did not propose/want to act/move
18 garden

Is by a forgèd process[19] of my death
Rankly abused.[20] But know, thou noble youth,
The serpent that did sting thy father's life
Now wears his crown.

40 *Hamlet*   O my prophetic soul!
My uncle!

Ghost Ay, that incestuous,[21] that adulterate[22] beast,
With witchcraft of his wit, with traitorous[23] gifts –
O wicked wit and gifts, that have the power
45 So to seduce! – won to his shameful lust
The will of my most seeming-virtuous queen.
O Hamlet, what a falling-off was there
From me, whose love was of that dignity[24]
That it went hand in hand even with[25] the vow
50 I made to her in marriage – and to decline[26]
Upon a wretch whose natural gifts were poor
To[27] those of mine!
But virtue, as it never will be moved,
Though lewdness court it in a shape of heaven,
55 So lust, though to a radiant angel[28] linked,
Will sate itself in a celestial bed,
And prey[29] on garbage.

---

19 story
20 corruptly/grossly deceived/imposed upon
21 see act 1, scene 2, note 88
22 adulterous
23 treacherous
24 excellence, worth, honor
25 exactly in accord/parallel with
26 sink, descend
27 compared to
28 Satan
29 feed

But soft! methinks I scent the morning air.
Brief let me be. Sleeping within my orchard,
My custom always of the afternoon,   60
Upon my secure[30] hour thy uncle stole,
With juice of cursed hebenon[31] in a vial,
And in the porches[32] of my ears did pour
The leperous distilment,[33] whose effect
Holds such an enmity[34] with blood of man   65
That swift as quicksilver it courses[35] through
The natural gates and alleys[36] of the body,
And with a sudden vigor it doth posset[37]
And curd, like eager[38] droppings into milk,
The thin[39] and wholesome blood. So did it mine,   70
And a most instant tetter barked[40] about,
Most lazar-like,[41] with vile and loathsome crust,
All my smooth body.
Thus was I, sleeping, by a brother's hand
Of[42] life, of crown, of queen, at once dispatched,[43]   75
Cut off even in the blossoms of my sin,

30 unsuspecting
31 a never precisely identified poisonous plant
32 vestibules, outer approaches to the ear
33 tainted distilled drops / liquid
34 hostility, hatred
35 runs, flows
36 openings / entrances and passages
37 strength / force it doth curdle
38 acrid, acidic
39 feeble, weak
40 pustule / scablike crustiness broke out / erupted
41 as in leprosy
42 "of" is used three times, in this line, in the sense of "from"
43 removed / dismissed by death

Unhouseled, disappointed, unaneled,[44]
No reckoning[45] made, but sent to my account
With all my imperfections[46] on my head.

80 O, horrible! O, horrible, most horrible!
If thou hast nature[47] in thee, bear[48] it not,
Let not the royal bed of Denmark be
A couch[49] for luxury and damnèd incest.
But howsoever thou pursuest this act,

85 Taint not thy mind, nor let thy soul contrive
Against thy mother aught. Leave her to heaven
And to those thorns that in her bosom lodge,
To prick and sting[50] her. Fare thee well at once!
The glow-worm[51] shows the matin to be near,

90 And 'gins to pale his uneffectual[52] fire.
Adieu, adieu, adieu. Remember me.

EXIT

Hamlet O all you host of heaven! O earth! What else?
And shall I couple[53] hell? O, fie! Hold,[54] hold, my heart,
And you, my sinews,[55] grow not instant old,

---

44 not having received communion, unprepared, not having received the
   sacrament of extreme unction
45 an account to God of one's life and conduct
46 faults, blemishes
47 natural human feeling / affection
48 tolerate, endure
49 (1) a bed; (2) an animal's lair
50 pierce, cut
51 firefly
52 now relatively ineffective light
53 add on
54 stand fast, stay steady
55 nerves, muscles, strength

But bear me stiffly[56] up. Remember thee?   95
Ay, thou poor ghost, while memory holds a seat
In this distracted globe.[57] Remember thee?
Yea, from the table[58] of my memory
I'll wipe away all trivial fond[59] records,
All saws of books,[60] all forms, all pressures[61] past,   100
That youth and observation copied there,
And thy commandment all alone shall live
Within the book and volume[62] of my brain,
Unmixed with baser matter.[63] Yes, by heaven!
O most pernicious woman!   105
O villain, villain, smiling, damnèd villain!
My tables[64] – meet[65] it is I set it down
That one may smile, and smile, and be a villain.
At least I am sure it may be so in Denmark.

HAMLET WRITES

So, uncle, there you are. Now to my word: 110
It is "Adieu, adieu, remember me."
I have sworn 't.

VOICES FROM WITHIN

56 firmly, resolutely
57 in his confused/perplexed/deranged skull
58 writing tablet, slate
59 unimportant/paltry, foolish
60 maxims/sayings/proverbs from books
61 shapes/images/impressions/stamps
62 record and mass
63 (1) substance; (2) thought, topic; (3) things written
64 writing tablets, slates
65 proper, fitting, appropriate★

Marcellus, Horatio My lord, my lord!

Marcellus   Lord Hamlet!

Horatio   Heavens

secure[66] him!

Hamlet So be it!

115 *Horatio* Hillo, ho, ho,[67] my lord!

Hamlet Hillo, ho, ho, boy! Come, bird, come.

ENTER HORATIO AND MARCELLUS

Marcellus How is't,[68] my noble lord?

Horatio   What news, my lord?

Hamlet O, wonderful!

Horatio Good my lord,[69] tell it.

Hamlet   No, you will reveal it.

Horatio Not I, my lord, by heaven.

120 *Marcellus*   Nor I, my lord.

Hamlet How say you, then? Would heart of man once[70] think
it?

But you'll be secret?

Horatio, Marcellus   Ay, by heaven, my lord.

Hamlet There's ne'er a villain dwelling in all Denmark (*pause*)
But he's an arrant knave.[71]

125 *Horatio* There needs no ghost, my lord, come from the grave
To tell us this.

Hamlet   Why, right, you are in the right —

66 protect, guard
67 a falconer's call to his bird
68 what's happened
69 my good lord
70 ever
71 downright / unmitigated / notorious rogue

And so, without more circumstance[72] at all,
I hold it fit that we shake hands and part,
You, as your business and desire shall point you;
For every man has business and desire,   130
Such as it is, and for mine own poor part,
Look you, I'll go pray.

Horatio These are but wild and whirling words, my lord.

Hamlet I am sorry they offend you – heartily.
Yes, 'faith, heartily.

Horatio   There's no offense, my lord.   135

Hamlet Yes, by Saint Patrick, but there is, Horatio,
And much offense, too. Touching this vision here,
It is an honest[73] ghost, that let me tell you.
For[74] your desire to know what is between us,
O'ermaster 't[75] as you may. And now, good friends,   140
As you are friends, scholars and soldiers,
Give me one poor[76] request.

Horatio What is't, my lord? We will.

Hamlet Never make known what you have seen to-night.

Horatio, Marcellus My lord, we will not.

Hamlet   Nay, but swear't.

Horatio   In faith,   145
My lord, not I.

Marcellus   Nor I, my lord, in faith.

Hamlet   Upon[77] my sword.

72 particulars, details
73 creditable, virtuous, respectable*
74 as for
75 overcome/conquer it
76 small, humble, insignificant
77 swear it upon

Marcellus   We have sworn, my lord, already.

Hamlet   Indeed,[78] upon my sword, indeed.

Ghost   (*beneath the stage*) Swear.

Hamlet   Ah, ha, boy! Say'st thou so? Art thou there,
150   Truepenny?[79]

Come on, you hear this fellow in the cellarage.

Consent to swear.

Horatio   Propose the oath, my lord.

Hamlet   Never to speak of this that you have seen.

Swear by my sword.

155 Ghost   (*beneath the stage*) Swear.

Hamlet   Hic et ubique?[80] Then we'll shift our ground.[81]

Come hither, gentlemen,

And lay your hands again upon my sword.

Swear by my sword

160   Never to speak of this that you have heard

Ghost   (*beneath the stage*) Swear by his sword.

Hamlet   Well said, old mole! Canst work i' the earth so fast?

A worthy pioner![82] Once more remove,[83] good friends.

Horatio   O day and night, but this is wondrous strange!

165 Hamlet   And therefore as a stranger[84] give it welcome.

There are more things in heaven and earth, Horatio,

Than are dreamt of in your philosophy.[85]

---

78 in truth
79 trustworthy/honest person
80 Here and everywhere/anywhere?
81 location
82 soldier armed with a shovel
83 change position
84 Horatio is a stranger in Denmark
85 the philosophy studied at the university where both have studied

But come.
Here, as before: never, so help you mercy,
How strange or odd some'er I bear myself[86] –   170
As I perchance hereafter shall think meet
To put an antic disposition on,[87]
That you, at such times seeing me, never shall,
With arms encumbered[88] – thus – or this headshake,
Or by pronouncing of some doubtful[89] phrase,   175
As "Well, well, we know," or "We could, an if we would,"
Or "If we list[90] to speak," or "There be, and if they might,"[91]
Or such ambiguous giving out,[92] to note
That you know aught of me – this do swear,
So grace and mercy at your most need[93] help you.   180
Ghost   (*beneath the stage*) Swear.

THEY SWEAR

Hamlet Rest, rest, perturbèd spirit! So, gentlemen,
With all my love I do commend me[94] to you,
And what so poor a man as Hamlet is
May do, to express his love and friending to you,   185
God willing, shall not lack. Let us go in together –

86 how strange or odd however I behave
87 to assume/pretend to a grotesque/fantastic/clownish mood
88 folded
89 questionable
90 wished
91 there be those who, if they could
92 saying, reporting, pronouncing
93 greatest need
94 entrust/commit myself

And still your fingers on your lips, I pray.
The time is out of joint.[95] O cursèd spite,[96]
That ever I was born to set it right!
190   Nay, come, let's go together.

EXEUNT

95 order
96 fortune

Act 2

SCENE I

A room

ENTER POLONIUS AND REYNALDO

Polonius   Give him this money[1] and these notes, Reynaldo.

Reynaldo   I will, my lord.

Polonius   You shall do marvell's[2] wisely, good Reynaldo,
   Before you visit him, to make inquire
   Of his behavior.

Reynaldo   My lord, I did intend it.   5

Polonius   Marry, well said; very well said. Look you, sir,
   Inquire me first what Danskers[3] are in Paris,
   And how, and who, what means,[4] and where they keep,[5]
   What company, at what expense,[6] and finding

1 these coins
2 marvelously
3 Danes
4 financial resources, money, wealth
5 reside, lodge
6 cost

53

10 By this encompassment[7] and drift[8] of question
That they do know my son, come you[9] more nearer
Than your particular demands[10] will touch it.
Take you,[11] as 'twere, some distant knowledge of him,
As thus: "I know his father and his friends,
15 And in part him." Do you mark this, Reynaldo?

Reynaldo Ay, very well, my lord.

Polonius "And in part him, but" – you may say – "not well:
But, if't be he I mean,[12] he's very wild,
Addicted[13] so and so." And there put on[14] him
20 What forgeries you please – marry, none so rank[15]
As may dishonor him. Take heed of that.
But, sir, such wanton, wild and usual slips[16]
As are companions noted and most known[17]
To youth and liberty.[18]

Reynaldo   As gaming,[19] my lord.

25 *Polonius* Ay, or drinking, fencing, swearing, quarrelling,
Drabbing[20] – you may go so far.

Reynaldo My lord, that would dishonor him.

7 circling about
8 purpose, plan
9 you will come
10 detailed questions / requests
11 assume
12 if this is the man I'm talking about
13 prone to
14 attribute to
15 foul
16 such undisciplined / frolicsome errors / blunders
17 things associated with and most familiar
18 unrestrained conduct, free opportunity
19 like gambling
20 whoring

Polonius 'Faith, no; as you may season it in the charge.[21]
  You must not put another scandal[22] on him,
  That he is open to incontinency.[23]   30
  That's not my meaning. But breathe his faults so quaintly[24]
  That they may seem the taints of liberty,
  The flash and outbreak of a fiery mind,
  A savageness in unreclaimèd[25] blood
  Of general assault.[26]
Reynaldo   But, my good lord –   35
Polonius Wherefore should you[27] do this?
Reynaldo   Ay, my lord,
  I would know that.
Polonius   Marry, sir, here's my drift,[28]
  And I believe, it is a fetch of warrant.[29]
  You laying these slight sullies on my son,
  As 'twere a thing a little soiled i' the working[30] –   40
  Mark you:
  Your party in converse,[31] him you would sound,[32]
  Having ever seen in the prenominate crimes[33]
  The youth you breathe of be guilty, be assured

21 adjust it in the accusation
22 rumor, injurious report
23 utter licentiousness
24 cleverly, cunningly
25 a wildness in unrestrained, uncultivated
26 universal onset
27 why are you supposed to
28 purpose, aim, goal
29 trick/contrivance that is justified
30 something that has become a little soiled, in performing some labor/process
31 person with whom you are conversing
32 the one you wish/want to probe
33 at any time having seen the youth you speak be guilty of the specified sins

45   He closes with you in this consequence,[34]

       "Good sir," or so,[35] or "friend," or "gentleman" –

       According to the phrase or the addition[36]

       Of man and country –

Reynaldo   Very good, my lord.

Polonius   And then, sir, does 'a this – 'a does –

50   What was I about to say? By the mass, I was

       About to say something! Where did I leave?

Reynaldo At "closes in the consequence," at "friend

       Or so" – and "gentleman."

Polonius   At "closes in the consequence," ay, marry;

55   He closes thus: "I know the gentleman;

       I saw him yesterday, or t' other day,

       Or then, or then, with such, or such, and, as you say,

       There was a' gaming, there o'ertook in's rouse,[37]

       There falling out[38] at tennis." Or perchance,

60   "I saw him enter such a house of sale,"[39]

       Videlicet,[40] a brothel, or so forth.

       See you now:[41]

       Your bait of falsehood takes this carp[42] of truth,

       And thus do we of wisdom and of reach,[43]

---

34 logical result, conclusion
35 something like that
36 form of address
37 I came upon him in his drinking bout / carousing
38 quarreling
39 place where commodities were sold cheaply
40 for example
41 think / take note
42 your bait of falsehood catches this fish
43 scheming, trickery

With windlasses[44] and with assays of bias,[45]   65
By indirections find directions out.
So by my former lecture and advice,[46]
Shall you my son. You have me,[47] have you not?

Reynaldo My lord, I have.

Polonius   God bye[48] ye, fare ye well.

Reynaldo Good my lord.   70

Polonius Observe his inclination in yourself.[49]

Reynaldo I shall, my lord.

Polonius And let him ply his music.[50]

Reynaldo   Well, my lord.

Polonius Farewell.

EXIT REYNALDO

ENTER OPHELIA

How now, Ophelia! What's the matter?

Ophelia O, my lord, my lord, I have been so affrighted!   75

Polonius With what, i' the name of God?

Ophelia My lord, as I was sewing in my closet,[51]
Lord Hamlet, with his doublet all unbraced,[52]

---

44 roundabout paths taken, in hunting, to surprise game animals
45 deliberately off-center attempts (for example, making a curved throw, in
    bowling, to hit something not as readily hittable by a straight throw)
46 discourse/lesson and counsel
47 you have understood me
48 redeem (some texts emend to "goodbye")
49 follow his propensities for yourself
50 (1) apply himself to/work at his music or (2) yield to his way of doing things
51 small private room
52 close-fitting body garment, all unfastened

No hat upon his head,[53] his stockings fouled,[54]

80   Ungarterèd, and down-gyved[55] to his ankle,

Pale as his shirt; his knees knocking each other;

And with a look so piteous in purpórt[56]

As if he had been loosèd out of hell

To speak of horrors – he comes before me.

Polonius Mad for[57] thy love?

85   *Ophelia*   My lord, I do not know;

But truly, I do fear it.

Polonius   What said he?

Ophelia He took me by the wrist and held me hard;

Then goes he to the length of all his arm[58]

And, with his other hand thus o'er his brow,

90   He falls to such perusal of my face

As 'a would draw it. Long stayed he so.

At last, a little shaking of mine arm,

And thrice his head thus waving up and down,

He raised a sigh so piteous[59] and profound

95   As it did seem to shatter all his bulk[60]

And end his being. That done, he lets me go,

And with his head over his shoulder turned,

He seemed to find his way without his eyes,

For out o' doors he went without their helps,

100   And, to the last, bended their light on me.

---

53 hats were worn universally and everywhere, indoors and out
54 disgraceful, dirty
55 hanging down
56 outward bearing, effect
57 as a result/because of
58 then he straightens out his arm
59 PITyus
60 body

Polonius Come, go with me. I will go seek the king.

This is the very ecstasy[61] of love,

Whose violent property fordoes itself[62]

And leads the will to desperate undertakings

As oft as any passion under heaven   105

That does afflict our natures. I am sorry.

What, have you given him any hard words of late?

Ophelia No, my good lord. But as you did command,

I did repel his letters and denied

His access to me.

Polonius   That hath made him mad.[63]   110

I am sorry that with better heed and judgment

I had not quoted him.[64] I feared he did but trifle,

And meant to wrack[65] thee — but beshrew my jealousy![66]

By heaven, it is as proper to our age

To cast[67] beyond ourselves[68] in our opinions   115

As it is common for the younger sort

To lack discretion. Come, go we to the king.

This must be known, which, being kept close, might move[69]

More grief to hide than hate to utter love.[70]

Come.   120

EXEUNT

61 frenzy, rapture, madness
62 whose violent nature ruins/destroys itself
63 crazed
64 care/attention and judgment I did not take notice of
65 ruin
66 a plague upon my mistrust
67 as peculiar/distinctive to older men to calculate
68 more than we are capable of
69 being kept from sight/secret might cause
70 more harm to be be hidden than it would cause hate to speak of love (as he and Ophelia are about to do, with the King)

SCENE 2

FLOURISH.[1] ENTER CLAUDIUS, GERTRUDE, ROSENCRANTZ, GUILDENSTERN, AND ATTENDANTS

Claudius Welcome, dear Rosencrantz and Guildenstern.
Moreover[2] that we much did long to see you,
The need we have to use you did provoke
Our hasty sending.[3] Something have you heard
5   Of Hamlet's transformation: so call it,
Sith nor th' exterior nor the inward man
Resembles that it was.[4] What it should be,
More than his father's death, that thus hath put[5] him
So much from th' understanding of himself,
10   I cannot dream of. I entreat you both,
That, being of so[6] young days brought up with him,
And sith so neighboured to his youth and havior,[7]
That you vouchsafe your rest[8] here in our court
Some little time, so by your companies
15   To draw him on to pleasures, and to gather,
So much as from occasion you may glean,[9]
Whether aught to us unknown afflicts him thus,

1 fanfare, usually of brass instruments
2 besides
3 to employ you gave rise to our hurried sending of a message/messenger
4 since neither the outer nor the inner man resembles what it was
5 thrust, pushed
6 from such
7 so close to his behavior/deportment
8 grant/bestow your stay
9 as much as from circumstances/the course of events you may gather/ pick up

That, opened,[10] lies within our remedy.[11]

Gertrude Good gentlemen, he hath much talked of you;

And sure I am two men there are not living   20

To whom he more adheres.[12] If it will please you

To show us so much gentry[13] and good will

As to expend your time with us awhile,

For the supply and profit[14] of our hope,

Your visitation shall receive such thanks   25

As fits a king's remembrance.

Rosencrantz   Both your Majesties

Might, by the sovereign power you have of[15] us,

Put your dread pleasures more into command

Than to entreaty.

Guildenstern   But we both obey,

And here give up ourselves, in the full bent,[16]   30

To lay our service freely at your feet,

To be commanded.

Claudius   Thanks, Rosencrantz and gentle Guildenstern.

Gertrude   Thanks, Guildenstern and gentle Rosencrantz.

And I beseech you instantly to visit   35

My too much changèd son. Go, some of you,

And bring these gentlemen where Hamlet is.

Guildenstern Heavens make our presence and our practices[17]

---

10 uncovered, exposed
11 ability to cure
12 remains attached to
13 generosity, courtesy
14 support/assistance and advantage/good
15 over
16 full inclination, propensity, willingness
17 actions, performance

Pleasant and helpful to him!
Gertrude   Ay, amen!

EXEUNT ROSENCRANTZ, GUILDENSTERN,
AND SOME ATTENDANTS

ENTER POLONIUS

40   *Polonius* The ambassadors from Norway, my good lord,
       Are joyfully returned.
       Claudius Thou still hast been the father of good news.
       Polonius Have I, my lord? Assure you, my good liege,
       I hold[18] my duty, as I hold[19] my soul,
45   Both to my God and to my gracious king –
       And I do think, or else this brain of mine
       Hunts not the trail of policy so sure[20]
       As it hath used to do, that I have found
       The very[21] cause of Hamlet's lunacy.
50   *Claudius* O, speak of that! That do I long to hear.
       Polonius Give first admittance to th' ambassadors.
       My news shall be the fruit[22] to that great feast.
       Claudius Thyself do grace[23] to them, and bring them in.

EXIT POLONIUS

       He tells me, my dear Gertrude, he hath found
55   The head[24] and source of all your son's distemper.[25]

18 abide by, observe
19 keep watch over
20 does not hunt the tracks/traces of diplomacy/statecraft as reliably/steadily
21 true, real★
22 dessert
23 favor
24 chief part
25 disordered/deranged condition, illness, disease

Gertrude   I doubt it is no other but the main,[26]
His father's death, and our o'erhasty marriage.
Claudius   Well, we shall sift[27] him.

ENTER POLONIUS, WITH VOLTIMAND AND CORNELIUS

                              Welcome, my good friends!
Say, Voltimand, what[28] from our brother Norway?
Voltimand   Most fair return of greetings and desires.[29]   60
Upon our first, he sent out[30] to suppress
His nephew's levies,[31] which to him appeared
To be a preparation 'gainst the Polack,
But better looked into, he truly found
It was against your highness. Whereat grieved,   65
That so his sickness, age and impotence
Was falsely borne in hand,[32] sends out arrests[33]
On Fortinbras; which he, in brief, obeys,
Receives rebuke from Norway, and in fine[34]
Makes vow before his uncle never more   70
To give the assay[35] of arms against your majesty.
Whereon old Norway, overcome with joy,
Gives him threescore thousand[36] crowns in annual fee[37]

26 the principal / essential / chief one
27 test, question, examine
28 what response / news
29 requests
30 upon our first interview / meeting, he sent out orders
31 enrollment of men as soldiers
32 alleged, pretended
33 orders to stop / halt
34 finally
35 make a trial
36 3,000 times 20 (a "score") = 60,000 monetary units of significant size, not readily converted to modern terms
37 annual payment, allotment

And his commission to employ those soldiers,
75 So levied as before, against the Polack —
With an entreaty, herein further shown,
(*giving a paper*)
That it might please you to give quiet pass[38]
Through your dominions for this enterprise,
On such regards of safety and allowance[39]
As therein are set down.
80 *Claudius*   It likes us well,[40]
And at our more considered time[41] we'll read,
Answer, and think upon this business.
Meantime, we thank you for your well-took[42] labour.
Go to your rest; at night we'll feast together.
Most welcome home!

EXEUNT VOLTIMAND AND CORNELIUS

85 *Polonius*   This business is well ended.
(*Polonius pauses*)
My liege, and madam, to expostulate[43]
What majesty should be, what duty is,
Why day is day, night night, and time is time,
Were nothing but to waste night, day, and time.
90 Therefore, since brevity is the soul of wit,[44]
And tediousness the limbs and outward flourishes,[45]

---

38 peaceful/untroubled passage
39 such particulars of safeguards and approval/permission
40 that much pleases me
41 when I have the time for more deliberate thought
42 usefully expended
43 discuss
44 reason, intelligence*
45 embellishments, florid expressions

I will be brief. Your noble son is mad.
Mad call I it; for to define true madness
What is't but to be nothing else but mad?
But let that go.
Gertrude   More matter,[46] with less art.[47]   95
Polonius Madam, I swear I use no art at all.
That he is mad, 'tis true: 'tis true 'tis pity;
And pity 'tis 'tis true — a foolish figure[48] —
But farewell it, for I will use no art.
Mad let us grant him, then. And now remains   100
That we find out the cause of this effect,[49]
Or rather say, the cause of this defect,
For this effect defective comes by cause.[50]
Thus it remains, and the remainder thus.
Perpend.[51]   105
I have a daughter — have while she is mine —
Who, in her duty and obedience, mark,
Hath given me this:
(shows a letter)
             Now gather, and surmise.[52]
(reads)
"To the celestial and my soul's idol, the most beautified
Ophelia" — That's an ill phrase, a vile phrase; "beautified"   110
Is a vile phrase — but you shall hear. Thus:

---

46 substance★
47 learning, acquired skills
48 figure of speech
49 result
50 happens because it is caused to happen
51 consider
52 now infer/deduce and conceive/imagine

"In her excellent[53] white bosom, these, &c."

Gertrude Came this from Hamlet to her?

Polonius Good madam, stay a while. I will be faithful.[54]

115 "Doubt thou the stars are fire;
Doubt that the sun doth move;
Doubt truth to be a liar;
But never doubt I love.

[handwritten note: Time of new discovery of the world]

"O dear Ophelia, I am ill at these numbers,[55]
120 I have not art to reckon[56] my groans. But that
I love thee best, O most best, believe it. Adieu.
'Thine evermore, most dear lady, whilst
this machine is[57] to him, HAMLET."

This, in obedience, hath my daughter shown me,
125 And, more above,[58] hath his solicitings,
As they fell out[59] by time, by means and place,
All given to mine ear.

Claudius   But how hath she
Received his love?

Polonius   What do you think of me?

Claudius As of a man faithful and honorable.

130 *Polonius* I would fain[60] prove so. But what might you think,
When I had seen this hot love on the wing —

53 exalted, honored
54 conscientious, reliable
55 unskilled/bad at this poetry
56 count, calculate
57 while this structure/body belongs
58 in addition
59 proceeded
60 rejoice to

As I perceived it, I must tell you that,
Before my daughter told me — what might you,
Or my dear Majesty your queen here, think,
If I had played the desk or table-book,[61]   135
Or given my heart a-winking,[62] mute and dumb,
Or looked upon this love with idle[63] sight?
What might you think? No, I went round[64] to work,
And my young mistress[65] thus I did bespeak:[66]
"Lord Hamlet is a prince, out of thy star;[67]   140
This must not be." And then I precepts gave her,
That she should lock herself from his resort,[68]
Admit no messengers, receive no tokens.[69]
Which done, she took the fruits of[70] my advice,
And he, repelled — a short tale to make —   145
Fell into a sadness, then into a fast,
Thence to a watch,[71] thence into a weakness,
Thence to a lightness,[72] and by this declension[73]
Into the madness wherein now he raves,
And all we[74] mourn for.

61 a book containing tablets used for writing memoranda
62 allowed my heart to wink (that is, closed his eyes)
63 trifling, lazy
64 thoroughly
65 lady
66 speak to
67 beyond your rank / social sphere
68 visits
69 gifts
70 she profited from
71 vigil, wakefulness
72 lightheadedness
73 declining, falling away
74 all of us

150 *Claudius* (*to Gertrude*) Do you think 'tis this?

 Gertrude It may be, very like.[75]

 Polonius Hath there been such a time, I would fain know that,

  That I have positively said " 'Tis so,"

  When it proved otherwise?

 Claudius   Not that I know.

 Polonius (*pointing to his head and shoulder*)

155 Take this from this, if this be otherwise.

  If circumstances[76] lead me, I will find

  Where truth is hid, though it were hid indeed

  Within the center.[77]

 Claudius   How may we try[78] it further?

 Polonius You know, sometimes he walks four hours together[79]

  Here in the lobby.[80]

160 *Gertrude*   So he does indeed.

 Polonius At such a time I'll loose my daughter to him.

  Be you and I behind an arras[81] then.

  Mark the encounter. If he love her not,

  And be not from his reason fall'n thereon,[82]

165 Let me be no assistant[83] for a state,

  But keep a farm and carters.[84]

---

75 likely, probably

76 facts, circumstantial evidence

77 the center of the earth

78 test, sift, examine

79 continuously, at a time

80 corridor

81 tapestry, hanging screen

82 because of that

83 aide

84 conduct/maintain a farm and cart drivers (meaning "mere" cart-drivers, or "low fellows, boors")

Claudius   We will try it.

ENTER HAMLET, READING

Gertrude But look where sadly[85] the poor wretch comes,
reading.

Polonius Away, I do beseech you, both away:
I'll board him presently.[86] O, give me leave![87]

EXEUNT CLAUDIUS, GERTRUDE, AND ATTENDANTS

How does my good Lord Hamlet?   170

Hamlet Well, God-a-mercy.

Polonius Do you know me, my lord?

Hamlet Excellent well. You are a fishmonger.[88]

Polonius Not I, my lord.

Hamlet Then I would you were so honest a man.   175

Polonius Honest, my lord!

Hamlet Ay, sir; to be honest, as this world goes, is to be one man
picked out of ten thousand

Polonius That's very true, my lord.

Hamlet For if the sun breed[89] maggots in a dead dog, being a   180
good[90] kissing carrion[91] – Have you a daughter?

85 soberly, gravely
86 on the spot, immediately
87 leave me
88 literally, one who sells fish. But "fish" = "flesh," and "monger" = "dealer/
trafficker in a disreputable trade": what Hamlet is saying, slyly, is that
Polonius is a pimp
89 if the sun hatch, produce (it was thought to make dead matter "give birth
to" living matter)
90 some texts have "god," referring to the sun-god
91 being good at kissing a dead body/rotting flesh/worthless flesh

Polonius I have, my lord.

Hamlet Let her not walk i' th' sun. Conception is a blessing: but as your daughter may conceive, friend, look to 't.[92]

185 *Polonius* (*aside*) How say you by that? Still harping on my daughter. Yet he knew me not at first. 'A said I was a fishmonger. 'A is far gone, far gone. And truly, in my youth I suffered much extremity[93] for love – very near this. I'll speak to him again. – What do you read, my lord?

190 *Hamlet* Words, words, words.

Polonius What is the matter, my lord?

Hamlet Between who?

Polonius I mean, the matter that you read, my lord.

Hamlet Slanders, sir, for the satirical rogue says here that old 195 men have grey beards, that their faces are wrinkled, their eyes purging thick amber[94] and plum-tree gum[95] and that they have a plentiful lack of wit, together with most weak hams.[96] All which, sir, though I most powerfully and potently[97] believe, yet I hold it not honesty to have it thus set down, for 200 yourself, sir, should be old as I am – if like a crab you could go backward.

Polonius (*aside*) Though this be madness, yet there is method in 't. Will you walk out of the air,[98] my lord?

Hamlet Into my grave.

205 *Polonius* Indeed, that is out o' the air. (*aside*) How pregnant

92 beware
93 severe urgency
94 their eyes leaking thick spermaceti (made from sperm whale oil)
95 resin, sap
96 muscles in the back of the thigh and buttocks
97 strongly, with good reason
98 the outside air (thought to be unhealthy for those who were ill)

sometimes his replies are! A happiness that often madness hits on, which reason and sanity could not so prosperously be delivered of. I will leave him, and suddenly contrive[99] the means of meeting between him and my daughter. – My honorable lord, I will most humbly take my leave of you. 210

Hamlet   You cannot, sir, take from me anything that I will more willingly part withal – except my life – except my life – except my life.

Polonius   Fare you well, my lord.

ENTER GUILDENSTERN AND ROSENCRANTZ

Hamlet   These tedious old fools! 215

Polonius   (leaving) You go to seek the Lord Hamlet? There he is.

Rosencrantz   (to Polonius) God save you,[100] sir!

EXIT POLONIUS

Guildenstern   My honored lord!

Rosencrantz   My most dear lord! 220

Hamlet   My excellent good friends! How dost thou, Guildenstern? Ah, Rosencrantz! Good lads, how do ye both?

Rosencrantz   As the indifferent[101] children of the earth.

Guildenstern   Happy, in that we are not over-happy. On Fortune's cap we are not the very button.[102] 225

Hamlet   Nor the soles of her shoe?

Rosencrantz   Neither, my lord.

99 instantly plan
100 a formal acknowledgment
101 unimportant
102 topmost ornament

Hamlet   Then you live about her waist, or in the middle of
her favors?[103]

230 *Guildenstern* 'Faith, her privates[104] we.

Hamlet   In the secret parts[105] of Fortune? O, most true! She
is a strumpet. What's the news?

Rosencrantz None, my lord, but that the world's grown honest.

Hamlet   Then is doomsday near: but your news is not true.

235 Let me question more in particular: what have you, my good
friends, deserved at the hands of Fortune, that she sends you
to prison hither?

Guildenstern Prison, my lord?

Hamlet   Denmark's a prison.

240 *Rosencrantz* Then is the world one.

Hamlet   A goodly [106] one; in which there are many
confines, wards,[107] and dungeons, Denmark being one o' the
worst.

Rosencrantz We think not so, my lord.

245 *Hamlet*   Why, then, 'tis none to you,[108] for there is nothing
either good or bad but thinking makes it so. To me it is a
prison.

Rosencrantz Why then, your ambition makes it one. 'Tis[109] too
narrow for your mind.

250 *Hamlet*   O God, I could be bounded in a nut shell and
count myself a king of infinite space, were it not that I have
bad dreams.

103 attractions, charms
104 low-ranking men / soldiers (*and* private parts / genitalia)
105 in the hidden / unseen regions / portions
106 large
107 places of confinement / prisons, divisions within a prison
108 it is not one to you
109 Denmark is

Guildenstern Which dreams indeed are ambition, for the very
substance of the ambitious is merely the shadow of a
dream.[110]   255

Hamlet   A dream itself is but a shadow.

Rosencrantz Truly, and I hold[111] ambition of so airy and light a
quality that it is but a shadow's shadow.

Hamlet   Then are our beggars bodies, and our monarchs
and outstretched[112] heroes but the beggars' shadows.[113] –   260
Shall we to the court? for, by my fay, I cannot reason.[114]

Rosencrantz, Guildenstern We'll wait upon you.[115]

Hamlet   No such matter: I will not sort[116] you with the rest
of my servants, for, to speak to you like an honest man, I am
most dreadfully attended.[117] But, in the beaten way[118] of   265
friendship, what make you at Elsinore?

Rosencrantz To visit you, my lord; no other occasion.[119]

Hamlet   Beggar that I am, I am even poor in thanks, but I
thank you – and sure, dear friends, my thanks are too dear a
halfpenny.[120] Were you not sent for? Is it your own inclining?   270

---

110 the dream precedes the substance: ambition dreams of what it does not yet
possess, and when (and if) it possess the dream, it has nothing more than its
"shadow" (the reflected image)
111 consider, think, believe
112 stretched out / overextended men of vast ambition (heroes can be great
shadows without any substance)
113 beggars, being unambitious, have substance rather than mere "dreams"
114 argue, discourse (as university students, which all three men were, had been
taught to do)
115 we will attend / serve you
116 classify
117 waited on, served
118 well-traveled road / path
119 cause, reason
120 too costly / expensive at a halfpenny

Is it a free[121] visitation? Come, deal justly with me. Come,
come. Nay, speak.

Guildenstern What should we say, my lord?

Hamlet Why, anything, but to the purpose.[122] You were
275 sent for, and there is a kind of confession in your looks which
your modesties[123] have not craft enough to color.[124] I know
the good king and queen have sent for you.

Rosencrantz To what end, my lord?

Hamlet That you must teach me. But let me conjure you,
280 by the rights of our fellowship,[125] by the consonancy[126] of
our youth, by the obligation of our ever-preserved love, and
by what more dear a better proposer could charge you
withal, be even[127] and direct with me, whether you were sent
for or no.

285 *Rosencrantz* (*aside to Guildenstern*) What say you?

Hamlet (*aside*) Nay, then, I have an eye of you.[128] — If you
love me, hold not off.

Guildenstern My lord, we were sent for.

Hamlet I will tell you why: so shall my anticipation prevent
290 your discovery,[129] and your secrecy to[130] the king and queen

---

121 voluntary, unrestricted
122 except on the subject being discussed
123 self-control/honesty of thought and feeling
124 skill/cunning enough to misrepresent, disguise
125 students were members of the "corporate" fellowship of a university
126 harmony, concord
127 what more precious someone better equipped to frame an argument could
lay upon/command you with, be straight
128 I am keeping an eye on you
129 revealing/disclosing it
130 being in the confidence of

moult[131] no feather. I have of late – but wherefore I know
not – lost my mirth, foregone all custom of exercise, and
indeed it goes so heavily with my disposition[132] that
this goodly frame,[133] the earth, seems to me a sterile
promontory,[134] this most excellent canopy,[135] the air, look   295
you, this brave o'erhanging firmament,[136] this majestical roof
fretted[137] with golden fire, why, it appears no other thing to
me than a foul and pestilent congregation of vapors.[138] What
a piece of work is a man, how noble in reason, how infinite in
faculties, in form and moving how express and admirable,[139]   300
in action how like an angel, in apprehension how like a god –
the beauty[140] of the world, the paragon[141] of animals! And
yet, to me, what is this quintessence[142] of dust? Man delights
not me – nor woman neither, though by your smiling you
seem to say so.   305

Rosencrantz My lord, there was no such stuff[143] in my thoughts.

Hamlet   Why did you laugh, then, when I said "man delights
not me"?

131 cause to fall off
132 sluggishly/laboriously/woefully with my mood/turn of mind
133 lovely/huge structure
134 barren projection of land, jutting out into the sea
135 shelter/covering
136 this splendid/handsome arch/vault of heaven
137 adorned
138 mass of exhalations (very negative connotation)
139 exact and to be wondered at/astonished by
140 ornament
141 supreme model
142 most essential essence
143 matter, rubbish, nonsense

Rosencrantz To think, my lord, if you delight not in man, what
310   lenten entertainment the players[144] shall receive from you.
       We coted[145] them on the way; and hither are they coming, to
       offer you service.[146]

Hamlet   He that plays the king shall be welcome; his majesty
       shall have tribute[147] of me; the adventurous knight shall use
315   his foil and target;[148] the lover shall not sigh gratis; the
       humorous[149] man shall end his part in peace; the clown shall
       make those laugh whose lungs are tickle o' the sere;[150] and
       the lady shall say her mind freely, or the blank verse shall
       halt[151] for't. What players[152] are they?

320 *Rosencrantz* Even those you were wont[153] to take delight in, the
       tragedians of the city.[154]

Hamlet   How chances it they travel? Their residence,[155]
       both in reputation and profit, was better both ways.

Rosencrantz I think their inhibition[156] comes by the means of
325   the late innovation.[157]

---

144 meager/dismal reception/welcome the actors
145 overtook, outstripped (a term used of hunting dogs)
146 their work/performance
147 homage, usually fiscal, paid to a king by one of his subjects; here used to
     mean "money"
148 small sword, blunt edged, with a button on the sharp point, and a small,
     round shield
149 odd, moody, capricious (that is, full of "humors")
150 loose/easy on the catch of a gun-lock (in current usage, "easy on the
     trigger")
151 go lame/limp, be defective
152 troop/company of actors
153 precisely those you were used/accustomed to
154 London
155 usual place (location and status)
156 prohibition? trouble? (see note 157, immediately below)
157 change, revolution, rebellion, insurrection (referring either to the success of

Hamlet   Do they hold the same estimation[158] they did when
I was in the city? Are they so followed?[159]

Rosencrantz No, indeed, are they not.

Hamlet   How comes it? Do they grow rusty?

Rosencrantz Nay, their endeavour keeps in the wonted pace,[160]   330
but there is, sir, an eyrie[161] of children, little eyases, that cry
out[162] on the top of question, and are most tyrannically
clapped[163] for't. These are now the fashion, and so berattle[164]
the common stages[165] – so they call them – that many
wearing rapiers[166] are afraid of goose-quills[167] and dare   335
scarce come thither.

Hamlet   What, are they children? Who maintains[168] 'em?
How are they escoted?[169] Will they pursue the quality[170] no
longer than they can sing?[171] Will they not say afterwards, if
they should grow themselves to common[172] players – as it is   340

---

the children's acting companies or the earl of Essex's rebellion; most
probably the former, in which case licensing problems could be the cause
of the "inhibition")

158 appreciation, esteem, reputation
159 in the same way attended / admired
160 usual course
161 a bird of prey's nest
162 young, untrained hawks / falcons (shrill-voiced and noisy) who exclaim /
   croak at the very highest level of speech
163 arbitrarily / vehemently applauded
164 rattle away at (in current usage, "put down")
165 the public (and adult) playhouses ("common": "low, vulgar")
166 who wear swords (as adult males of any standing did)
167 pens (wielded by those who support the children's acting companies)
168 supports, sustains
169 paid for (maintained)
170 profession, occupation
171 that is, once their boy soprano voices change
172 to become standard / adult

most like, if their means are no better[173] – their writers do them wrong to make them exclaim against their own succession?[174]

Rosencrantz 'Faith, there has been much to do[175] on both sides,
345 and the nation holds it no sin to tarre[176] them to controversy. There was, for a while, no money bid for argument,[177] unless the poet and the player went to cuffs[178] in the question.

Hamlet Is't possible?

Guildenstern O, there has been much throwing about of brains.

350 *Hamlet* Do the boys carry it away?[179]

Rosencrantz Ay, that they do, my lord – Hercules and his load[180] too.

Hamlet It is not very strange, for mine uncle is King of Denmark, and those that would make mouths[181] at him
355 while my father lived, give twenty, forty, fifty, an hundred ducats[182] a-piece for his picture in little.[183] 'Sblood,[184] there is something in this more than natural, if philosophy[185] could find it out.

---

173 no better than other adults/adult actors
174 line of succession
175 fuss
176 incite, provoke, irritate
177 offered for subjects/themes
178 blows
179 gain the day, triumph
180 that is, the world: having sent Atlas to fetch the golden apples of the Hesperides, in Atlas's absence Hercules held up the world; the Globe Theatre had a sign showing Hercules with the "globe" on his shoulders
181 grimaces
182 gold coins
183 in miniature
184 God's blood (an oath)
185 wisdom, knowledge

A FLOURISH OF TRUMPETS[186]

Guildenstern There are the players.

Hamlet (*to Rosencrantz and Guildenstern*) Gentlemen, you   360
are welcome to Elsinore. Your hands, come then: th'
appurtenance of welcome is fashion and ceremony.[187] Let
me comply[188] with you in this garb, lest my extent[189] to the
players, which, I tell you, must show fairly[190] outwards,
should more appear like entertainment[191] than yours.[192] You   365
are welcome. — But my uncle-father and aunt-mother are
deceived.

Guildenstern In what, my dear lord?

Hamlet I am but mad north-north-west. When the wind is
southerly I know a hawk[193] from a handsaw.[194]   370

ENTER POLONIUS

Polonius Well be[195] with you, gentlemen!

Hamlet Hark you, Guildenstern, and you[196] too: at each

---

186 traveling actors thus introduced themselves, when arriving in a new locale
187 that which belongs to/is properly an accessory to the act of welcoming
someone (manners, custom, gestures, actions) involves the proper
observance of respectful forms of behavior
188 observe the forms of civility/politeness/courtesy
189 in this style/manner, lest my scope/degree of welcome
190 clearly, distinctly
191 hospitality, welcoming
192 your welcome (to Elsinore)
193 quadrangular tool, with a handle, used by plasterers (also a bird trained for
hunting)
194 one-handed saw
195 may it be well
196 Rosencrantz

ear a hearer.[197] That great baby you see there is not yet out of his swaddling-clouts.[198]

375 *Rosencrantz* Happily[199] he's the second time come to them, for they say an old man is twice[200] a child.

Hamlet I will prophesy he comes to tell me of the players. Mark it. – You say right, sir.[201] A Monday morning, 'twas so indeed.

380 *Polonius* My lord, I have news to tell you.

Hamlet My lord, I have news to tell you. When Roscius[202] was an actor in Rome –

Polonius The actors are come hither, my lord.

Hamlet Buzz, buzz.

385 *Polonius* Upon mine honor –

Hamlet Then came each actor on his ass[203] –

Polonius The best actors in the world, either for tragedy, comedy, history, pastoral, pastoral-comical, historical-pastoral, tragical-historical, tragical-comical-historical-pastoral, scene 390 individable,[204] or poem unlimited.[205] Seneca[206] cannot be

197 Hamlet here lowers his voice, to prevent Polonius from hearing, and warns Guildenstern and Rosencrantz to listen carefully
198 narrow, protective bandages wound around newborn infants, to prevent free movement
199 haply, perhaps★
200 for the second time
201 Hamlet invents a supposedly ongoing conversation
202 famous Roman comic actor
203 donkey
204 observing the classically derived three unities – place, time, and scene/setting
205 play free from restrictions (for example, the three unities)
206 Roman philosopher and author of distinctly rhetorical, often melodramatic tragedies

too heavy, nor Plautus[207] too light. For the law of writ[208] and the liberty,[209] these are the only men.

Hamlet O Jephthah,[210] judge of Israel, what a treasure hadst thou!

Polonius What a treasure had he, my lord?   395

Hamlet Why,

"One fair daughter and no more,

The which he lovèd passing well."

Polonius (*aside*) Still on my daughter.

Hamlet Am I not i' the right, old Jephthah?   400

Polonius If you call me Jephthah, my lord, I have a daughter that I love passing well.

Hamlet Nay, that follows[211] not.

Polonius What follows, then, my lord?

Hamlet Why, "As by lot, God wot,"[212] and then, you know, "It   405
came to pass, as most like it was." The first row of the pious
chanson[213] will show you more – for look here my
abridgement[214] comes.

ENTER FOUR OR FIVE PLAYERS

207 Roman comic playwright
208 something written (*and / or* a legal document: the sense is obscure)
209 whether what these actors put on is conservative-classical or less-
   conservative-classical (?)
210 who sacrificed his daughter, most unwillingly – and accidentally – to
   fulfill a vow (see Judges 11)
211 Polonius having a daughter, as Jepthah did, does not necessarily mean that,
   like Jepthah, he loves her exceedingly well; after all, the Bible describes
   Jepthah as a "mighty man"
212 as by chance/fortune, God knows: Hamlet quotes, as he did a few lines
   earlier, from a then-familiar ballad, "Jepthah, Judge of Israel"
213 line of the devout/faithful song
214 those who will wile away the time for Hamlet

81

You are welcome, masters[215] – welcome, all. I am glad to see
410 thee well. Welcome, good friends. O, old friend! Why, thy face
is valenced[216] since I saw thee last. Com'st thou to beard me
in Denmark? What, my young lady[217] and mistress! By'r[218]
lady, your ladyship is nearer to heaven[219] than when I saw
you last, by the altitude of a chopine.[220] Pray God, your
415 voice, like a piece of uncurrent gold,[221] be not cracked
within the ring.[222] – Masters, you are all welcome. We'll e'en
to't[223] like French falconers,[224] fly at any thing we see. We'll
have a speech straight.[225] Come, give us a taste of your
quality.[226] Come, a passionate speech.
420 *First Player* What speech, my lord?
    Hamlet   I heard thee speak me a speech once, but it was
never acted, or, if it was, not above[227] once, for the play, I
remember, pleased not the million.[228] 'Twas caviare to the

215 distinguished artists, models of their art (and possibly also learned men,
     worthy of the Master of Arts [M.A.] degree)
216 draped, bordered, fringed (the actor thus addressed now has a beard)
217 a boy: no women appeared in public on the Elizabethan stage
218 by our
219 closer (the boy has grown taller)
220 height of a shoe with thick sole, often of cork
221 valid / acceptable / legal coin of gold
222 from the coin's outer edge all the way through to the circle / ring set
     around the king's head (the crack shows that some of the gold had been
     clipped away); Hamlet puns on the "ring" (sound) of a voice
223 we'll go directly / straight / at once to it
224 a slur on French, as opposed to English, falconers / huntsmen using falcons
225 correctly done, recited all the way through
226 art
227 not more than
228 the multitude, the crowd

general,[229] but it was – as I received[230] it, and others, whose
judgments in such matters cried in the top of[231] mine – an   425
excellent play, well digested[232] in the scenes, set down with as
much modesty as cunning.[233] I remember one[234] said there
were no sallets[235] in the lines to make the matter savory, nor
no matter in the phrase[236] that might indict[237] the author of
affectation, but called it an honest method, as wholesome as   430
sweet, and, by very much, more handsome than fine.[238] One
speech in't I chiefly loved. 'Twas Aeneas' tale to Dido, and
thereabout of it[239] especially where he speaks of Priam's
slaughter. If it live in your memory, begin at this line – let me
see, let me see –   435

"The rugged Pyrrhus, like th' Hyrcanian beast"[240] –

'Tis not so[241] – It begins with Pyrrhus –

"The rugged[242] Pyrrhus, he whose sable arms,[243]

---

229 caviar was then new to England and not widely popular with the general
    public/multitude
230 accepted, regarded, believed, understood
231 were strongly uttered and above/better than
232 divided, arranged
233 as much control as skill, cleverness, art
234 someone
235 savory ingredients (from "salads")
236 style, language, diction
237 charge, accuse
238 suitable/apt/reliable rather than fashionable/elegant/ornamented
239 somewhere near where
240 the tiger
241 it does not go like that
242 rough, unpolished, harsh
243 black armor

Black as his purpose, did the night resemble
440 When he lay couchèd[244] in th' ominous horse,[245]
Hath now this dread and black complexion[246] smeared
With heraldry more dismal.[247] Head to foot
Now is he total gules,[248] horridly tricked[249]
With blood of fathers, mothers, daughters, sons,
445 Baked and impasted with the parching[250] streets,
That lend a tyrannous[251] and a damnèd light
To their lord's[252] murder. Roasted in wrath and fire,
And thus o'er-sized with coagulate gore,[253]
With eyes like carbuncles,[254] the hellish Pyrrhus
450 Old grandsire[255] Priam seeks."
So, proceed you.

Polonius 'Fore God, my lord, well spoken, with good
accent[256] and good discretion.

First Player "Anon[257] he finds him,
455 Striking too short[258] at Greeks. His ántique sword,
Rebellious[259] to his arm, lies where it falls,

244 lying in ambush
245 of ill omen, indicative of disaster-to-come Trojan horse
246 appearance
247 armorial signs/symbols more prophetic of disastrous, calamitous
248 stained red
249 adorned, decked
250 and encrusted with the hot, dry, scorching
251 oppressive, severe
252 Priam, king of Troy: the murder is just about to occur
253 covered over with clotted/congealed blood
254 sapphires and other reddish precious stones
255 grandfather, forefather
256 emphasis, stress
257 soon*
258 with limited/inadequate reach
259 resistant

Repugnant[260] to command. Unequal matched,
Pyrrhus at Priam drives,[261] in rage strikes wide,
But with the whiff and wind of his fell[262] sword
Th' unnervèd[263] father[264] falls. Then senseless Ilium,[265]   460
Seeming to feel this blow, with flaming top[266]
Stoops to his base,[267] and with a hideous crash
Takes prisoner Pyrrhus' ear.[268] For lo, his sword,
Which was declining on the milky[269] head
Of reverend[270] Priam, seemed i' the air to stick.[271]   465
So as a painted tyrant[272] Pyrrhus stood,
And like a neutral to his will and matter[273]
Did nothing.
But as we often see, against[274] some storm,
A silence in the heavens, the rack[275] stand still,   470
The bold winds speechless and the orb[276] below

---

260 hostile, antagonistic
261 rushes, hurries, dashes
262 but because of the gust and rush of air of his savage / cruel / relentless
263 enfeebled, incapable
264 Hector's father, among others
265 the fortress of Troy, incapable of feeling / perception
266 the Greeks have set fire to the fortress, and at this moment, its "flaming"
    heights collapse
267 descends to its foundation
268 the sound is so overwhelming that Pyrrhus's ear is taken captive: he is
    literally stunned, for a moment
269 falling on the white / gentle
270 aged and venerable
271 to be rendered immobile / fixed
272 like a painting of a villain / despot
273 like a noncombatant, someone indifferent / uninvolved in his business /
    occupation
274 drawing toward, in preparation for
275 clouds
276 globe / earth

As hush as death, anon the dreadful thunder
Doth rend the region,[277] so after Pyrrhus' pause
Arousèd vengeance sets him new a-work,
475 And never did the Cyclops'[278] hammers fall
On Mars's armor, forged for proof eterne,[279]
With less remorse than Pyrrhus' bleeding sword
Now falls on Priam.
Out, out, thou strumpet Fortune! All you gods
480 In general synod[280] take away her power;
Break all the spokes and fellies[281] from her wheel,
And bowl the round nave[282] down the hill of heaven,
As low as to the fiends!"

Polonius   This is too long.

485 Hamlet   It shall to the barber's, with your beard. – Prithee,
say on. He's for a jig[283] or a tale of bawdry, or[284] he sleeps. Say
on: come to Hecuba.[285]

First Player "But who, O, who had seen the mobled[286] queen – "

Hamlet   "The mobled queen?"

490 Polonius   That's good. "Mobled queen" is good.

277 the heavens / air
278 one-eyed giants, sons of Uranus
279 eternal invulnerability / impenetrability
280 assembly of your entire ranks
281 the curved pieces composing the outer rim of the wheel
282 hub
283 in for of a lively, comical performances at intermissions or at the end of a
     play
284 or else
285 old Priam's wife, the queen of Troy
286 having the face or head muffled

First Player "– Run barefoot up and down, threat'ning the
　　flames
　　With bisson rheum;[287] a clout upon that head
　　Where late the diadem[288] stood, and for a robe
　　About her lank and all o'er-teemèd loins,[289]
　　A blanket, in the alarm of fear caught up –　　　　　　495
　　Who this had seen, with tongue in venom steeped[290]
　　'Gainst Fortune's state would treason have pronounced.[291]
　　But if the gods themselves did see her, then
　　When she saw Pyrrhus make malicious sport
　　In mincing with his sword her husband's limbs,　　　500
　　The instant burst of clamor[292] that she made,
　　Unless things mortal move them not at all
　　Would have made milch[293] the burning eyes of heaven,
　　And passion[294] in the gods."

Polonius　　Look, whe'r[295] he has not turned his color, and has　505
　　tears in's eyes. Prithee, no more.

Hamlet　　'Tis well. I'll have thee speak out the rest of this
　　soon. (*to Polonius*) Good my lord, will you see the players well

---

287 blinding tears (the vast flow of which might extinguish the fires)
288 a piece of cloth/rag upon that head on which recently the crown
289 shrunken/flabby and overbred genitals (having experienced an excess of
　　child-bearing)
290 have spoken bitter/virulent words
291 against Fortune's greatness/power have treason spoken
292 outcry, din
293 pour like a nursemaid's milk ("milch": pronounced "miltch")
294 would have made/created passion ("intense feelings")
295 whether

bestowed?[296] Do you hear, let them be well used, for they are
the abstract[297] and brief chronicles of the time. After your
death you were better have a bad epitaph than their ill report
while you live.

510

Polonius   My lord, I will use them according to their desert.[298]

Hamlet   God's bodkin,[299] man, much better! Use every man
after[300] his desert, and who shall 'scape whipping?[301] Use
them after your own honor and dignity. The less they deserve,
the more merit is in your bounty.[302] Take[303] them in.

515

Polonius   Come, sirs.

Hamlet   Follow him, friends. We'll hear a play to-morrow.
(*aside to First Player*) Dost thou hear me, old friend; can you
play "The Murder of Gonzago"?

520

First Player Ay, my lord.

Hamlet   We'll ha't to-morrow night. You could, for a need,
study a speech of some dozen or sixteen lines, which I would
set down and insert in't, could you not?

525

First Player Ay, my lord.

Hamlet   Very well. Follow that lord — and look you mock
him not.

EXIT POLONIUS WITH ALL THE PLAYERS

296 put up, lodged
297 compendium, summary
298 deserving
299 God's dear body
300 according to
301 vagabonds were, by law, sentenced to whipping; traveling actors were often
    so accused and punished
302 virtue, kindness, generosity
303 escort, lead

(to Rosencrantz and Guildenstern) My good friends, I'll leave
you till night. You are welcome to Elsinore.   530
Rosencrantz   Good my lord!

Hamlet   Ay, so. God be w' ye.[304] – Now I am alone.
O, what a rogue and peasant[305] slave[306] am I!
Is it not monstrous that this player here,
But in a fiction, in a dream of passion,   535
Could force his soul so to his own conceit[307]
That from her working all his visage wanned,[308]
Tears in his eyes, distraction in's aspéct,[309]
A broken voice, and his whole function suiting[310]
With forms[311] to his conceit? And all for nothing!   540
For Hecuba!
What's Hecuba to him, or he to Hecuba,
That he should weep for her? What would he do,
Had he the motive and the cue for passion
That I have? He would drown the stage with tears   545
And cleave the general ear[312] with horrid speech,
Make mad the guilty and appal the free,[313]

304 "w' ye" = "with you" (a plural form of "you")
305 low fellow, rustic, boor, clown
306 servile rascal
307 imagination, conception
308 became pale, sickly
309 madness/confusion in his face/countenance
310 physical bearing adapted/falling in with
311 physical/bodily expressions
312 split/pierce the public ear
313 guiltless

Confound the ignorant, and amaze[314] indeed
The very faculties[315] of eyes and ears.
550 Yet I,
A dull and muddy-mettled[316] rascal, peak
Like John-a-dreams,[317] unpregnant of[318] my cause,
And can say nothing – no, not for a king,
Upon whose property and most dear life
555 A damned defeat[319] was made. Am I a coward?
Who calls me villain?[320] Breaks my pate across?[321]
Plucks off my beard, and blows it in my face?
Tweaks me by the nose? Gives me the lie i' the throat
As deep as to the lungs?[322] Who does me this?
560 Ha!
'Swounds,[323] I should take it, for it cannot be
But I am pigeon-livered and lack gall[324]
To make oppression bitter, or ere this
I should ha' fatted all the region kites[325]
565 With this slave's offal.[326] Bloody, bawdy villain!

314 put to shame the ignorant and astound/overwhelm with wonder indeed
315 even the faithful powers/capacities
316 and vague/confused
317 slink/droop like a proverbial dreamy fellow
318 not spurred on by
319 damned undoing, destruction, ruin
320 a base, low-born man
321 cracks/lays open my head from one side to the other
322 calls me a liar of profound, unmitigated proportions, a liar down to my very depths
323 God's (Jesus') wounds
324 meek/mild-tempered: pigeons were thought to lack "gall," or bile, a liver secretion, and therefore to be devoid of the spirit/capacity to resent insult/injury
325 hawks (and other scavenger birds) of the air/in the skies
326 this contemptible rascal [the King]'s entrails/intestines

Remorseless, treacherous, lecherous, kindless[327] villain!
O, vengeance!
Why, what an ass am I! This is most brave,[328]
That I, the son of a dear father murdered,
Prompted to my revenge by heaven and hell,   570
Must like a whore unpack[329] my heart with words,
And fall a-cursing like a very drab,[330]
A scullion!
Fie upon't, foh! About,[331] my brains!
Hum –   575
I have heard that guilty creatures sitting at a play
Have by the very cunning[332] of the scene
Been struck so to the soul that presently[333]
They have proclaimed their malefactions.[334]
For murder, though it have no tongue, will speak   580
With most miraculous organ.[335] I'll have these players
Play something like the murder of my father
Before mine uncle. I'll observe his looks,
I'll tent him to the quick.[336] If he but blench,[337]
I know my course. The spirit that I have seen   585
May be a devil, and the devil hath power

327 unnatural, devoid of natural feeling
328 courageous, splendid
329 open, unload
330 whore
331 attend to it, do it (?) or turn about/go in the opposite direction (?)
332 skill, cleverness
333 at once, promptly*
334 evil doings
335 means of action/operation
336 probe him to the central/vital/most sensitive part
337 flinch, start

T' assume a pleasing shape — yea, and perhaps
Out of[338] my weakness and my melancholy,
As he is very potent with such spirits,[339]
590   Abuses[340] me to damn me. I'll have grounds
More relative[341] than this. The play's the thing
Wherein I'll catch[342] the conscience of the king.

EXIT

338 from, because of
339 he is very powerful/effective with such emotions (that is, weakness and
    melancholy)
340 ill-uses, wrongs
341 reasons more credible/substantial
342 surprise, ensnare, lay hold of

Act 3

SCENE I

The castle

ENTER CLAUDIUS, GERTRUDE, POLONIUS, OPHELIA,
ROSENCRANTZ, AND GUILDENSTERN

Claudius   And can you, by no drift of conference,[1]
Get from him why he puts on[2] this confusion,
Grating so harshly[3] all his days of quiet
With turbulent and dangerous[4] lunacy?

Rosencrantz   He does confess he feels himself distracted,[5]
But from what cause he will by no means speak.

Guildenstern   Nor do we find him forward to be sounded,[6]
But with a crafty[7] madness keeps aloof

5

---

1 purposeful direction of speech
2 assumes (either honestly or deceptively)
3 irritating so disagreeably, unpleasingly
4 with violent and risky, injurious
5 perplexed, confused, mentally unstable
6 eager to be questioned, examined
7 skillful, ingenious

When we would bring him on to[8] some confession
Of his true state.

10 *Gertrude*   Did he receive you well?

Rosencrantz Most like a gentleman.

Guildenstern But with much forcing[9] of his disposition.

Rosencrantz Niggard of question,[10] but of our demands[11]
Most free in his reply.

Gertrude   Did you assay him
15 To any pastime?[12]

Rosencrantz Madam, it so fell out[13] that certain players
We o'er-raught[14] on the way. Of these we told him,
And there did seem in him a kind of joy
To hear of it. They are about[15] the court
20 And, as I think, they have already order[16]
This night to play before him.

Polonius   'Tis most true,
And he beseeched me to entreat your majesties
To hear and see the matter.[17]

Claudius   With all my heart, and it doth much content me
25 To hear him so inclined.
Good gentlemen, give him a further edge[18]

8 persuade/induce him to
9 strain, effort
10 stingy of talk/speech
11 questions
12 tempt him to any amusement, entertainment, sport
13 chanced to happen
14 overtook, came past
15 around, near
16 an order
17 thing, business
18 keenness of desire

And drive his purpose[19] into these delights.
Rosencrantz   We shall, my lord.

EXEUNT ROSENCRANTZ AND GUILDENSTERN

Claudius   Sweet Gertrude, leave us too,
For we have closely [20] sent for Hamlet hither,
That he, as 'twere by accident, may here   30
Affront[21] Ophelia.
Her father and myself, lawful espials,[22]
Will so bestow[23] ourselves that, seeing, unseen,
We may of their encounter frankly judge
And gather by him, as he is behaved,   35
If 't be th' affliction[24] of his love or no
That thus he suffers for.
Gertrude   I shall obey you.
And for your part, Ophelia, I do wish
That your good beauties [25] be the happy[26] cause
Of Hamlet's wildness. So shall I hope your virtues   40
Will bring him to his wonted way[27] again,
To both your honors.
Ophelia   Madam, I wish it may.

EXIT GERTRUDE

19 propel/urge on his intention, determination, resolution
20 privately, secretly
21 meet face to face with
22 permissible/justifiable/legitimate spies
23 locate, stow away
24 pain, calamity
25 including both her visual and her intellectual and moral beauties
26 fortunate, blessed
27 usual/customary path, manner

Polonius Ophelia, walk you here.[28] – Gracious,[29] so[30] please you,

We will bestow ourselves. (*to Ophelia*) Read on this book,[31]

45 That show of such an exercise may color[32]

Your loneliness. We are oft to blame[33] in this:

'Tis too much proved that with devotion's visage[34]

And pious action we do sugar o'er

The devil himself.

Claudius (*aside*) O, 'tis too true!

50 How smart a lash that speech doth give my conscience!

The harlot's cheek, beautied with plastering art,

Is not more ugly to the thing[35] that helps it

Than is my deed to my most painted[36] word.

O heavy burden!

55 *Polonius* I hear him coming. Let's withdraw, my lord.

EXEUNT CLAUDIUS AND POLONIUS

ENTER HAMLET (THINKING HIMSELF ALONE)

Hamlet To be, or not to be: that is the question. To live; to die?

Whether 'tis nobler in the mind to suffer[37]

---

28 off to the very side of the stage: Elizabethan theatrical convention made her inconspicuous – almost invisible – and, while thus placed, not a participant in the action or discourse, which she cannot hear

29 my gracious King

30 if it

31 read in a book of a visibly religious nature

32 that the appearance/display of such an act of devotion may make plausible/believable

33 at fault

34 face, false appearance

35 ugly to the unpainted/natural beauty (which remains primary)

36 my deed compared to my most pretended, artificial

37 endure, submit to, be damaged/pained/destroyed by

r he'll
d them The slings and arrows of outrageous fortune,[38]
death Or to take arms against a sea of troubles, *He knows he'll*
And by opposing end them? To die, to sleep *fail but he's* 60
No more, and by a sleep to say we end *going to try.*
The heart-ache and the thousand natural shocks
That flesh is heir to. 'Tis a consummation *union with*
Devoutly to be wished.[39] To die, to sleep – *Death (sexual)*
To sleep, perchance to dream: ay, there's the rub,[40]   65
For in that sleep of death what[41] dreams may come
When we have shuffled off[42] this mortal coil[43]
Must give us pause. There's the respect[44]
That makes calamity of so[45] long life –
For who would bear the whips and scorns[46] of time,   70
The oppressor's wrong,[47] the proud man's contumely,[48]
Betrayed The pangs of despisèd[49] love, the law's delay, *justice is at*
Corrupt The insolence of office[50] and the spurns[51]   *loss*
government That patient merit of th' unworthy takes,[52]
When he himself might his quietus[53] make   75

38 of excessive, furious, violent, cruel fortune
39 a completion/conclusion/end devoutly to be wished for
40 obstacle, difficulty
41 what kind of
42 "shuffled off" = "removed, gotten rid of"
43 when we have gotten rid of this clutter/fuss (*and* coil of rope/cable)
44 issue, matter, point, detail
45 a calamity of such a
46 lashes/thrusts (rapid movements in fencing) and mockery/contempt
47 wrongdoing
48 the arrogant/lordly/exalted man's insolent/insulting abuse
49 some texts have "desprized," meaning "unvalued"
50 officeholders, officialdom
51 disdainful/contemptuous rejections
52 common/ordinary person receives/endures
53 discharge from debt/life

With a bare bodkin?[54] Who would fardels[55] bear,
To grunt and sweat under a weary life,
But that the dread of something after death,
The undiscovered country from whose bourn[56]
80 No traveller returns, puzzles[57] the will
And makes us rather bear those ills we have
Than fly to others that we know not of?

aware;
guider

Thus conscience[58] does make cowards of us all,
And thus the native hue[59] of resolution

clouded
85 Is sicklied o'er with the pale cast[60] of thought,
lost
And enterprises[61] of great pitch and moment[62]
With this regard their currents turn awry[63]

could go wrong
(current doesn't
flow straight)

And lose the name of action. − Soft you now,
The fair Ophelia![64] − Nymph, in thy orisons[65]
Be all my sins remembered.

or
curret will take
where you need
to go.

90 *Ophelia*   Good my lord,
How does your honor for this many a day?[66]

54 dagger
55 burdens of sin/sorrow
56 unknown country from whose borders/boundaries
57 overwhelms, confounds
58 consciousness, inner knowledge/thought (*and* awareness of moral considerations)
59 natural color/appearance
60 shade
61 tasks, work
62 great height (a term from falconry: the moment before the falcon swoops down) and importance/weight
63 from/because of this consideration turn their active movement (as of a flowing stream) crooked/out of the right path/perverted/wrong
64 the probable course of events is that (1) he sees her, and (2) he approaches and speaks to her
65 maiden/damsel, in your prayers (Hamlet recognizes the nature of her book)
66 considering how long it has been since she has seen him

Hamlet I humbly thank you.[67] Well, well, well.[68]

Ophelia My lord, I have remembrances[69] of yours,

  That I have longèd long to re-deliver.

  I pray you now receive them.

Hamlet   No, not I   95

  I never gave you aught.

Ophelia My honored lord, you know right well you did,

  And with them words of so sweet breath composed[70]

  As made the things more rich. Their perfume lost,

  Take these again, for to the noble[71] mind   100

  Rich gifts wax poor when givers prove unkind.

  There, my lord.

SHE GIVES HIM BACK HIS GIFTS

Hamlet Ha, ha! Are you honest?

Ophelia My lord?

Hamlet Are you fair?[72]   105

Ophelia What means your lordship?

Hamlet That if you be honest and fair, your honesty should
  admit no discourse to[73] your beauty.

Ophelia Could beauty, my lord, have better commerce[74] than
  with honesty?   110

Hamlet Ay, truly; for the power of beauty will sooner transform

67 a very formal, aloof acknowledgment
68 in part an answer to her query?
69 keepsakes, tokens, gifts
70 in such sweet speech / volition / will, written
71 idealistic, highly moral
72 beautiful
73 should allow / receive no familiar intimacy with
74 dealings

honesty from what it is to a bawd[75] than the force of honesty
can translate beauty into his likeness.[76] This was sometime a
paradox,[77] but now the time gives it proof.[78] I did love you
115   once.

Ophelia Indeed, my lord, you made me believe so.

Hamlet You should not have believed me, for virtue cannot so
inoculate our old stock[79] but we shall relish of it.[80] I loved
you not.

120 Ophelia I was the more deceived.

Hamlet Get thee to a nunnery. Why wouldst thou be a breeder
of sinners? I am myself indifferent[81] honest, but yet I could
accuse me of such things that it were better my mother had
not borne me. I am very proud, revengeful, ambitious, with
125   more offences at my beck[82] than I have thoughts to put them
in, imagination to give them shape, or time to act them in.
What should such fellows as I do,[83] crawling between earth
and heaven? We are arrant knaves,[84] all: believe none of us.
Go thy ways to a nunnery. Where's your father?

130 Ophelia At home, my lord.

Hamlet Let the doors be shut upon him, that he may play the
fool nowhere but in's own house. Farewell.

Ophelia O, help him, you sweet heavens!

75 pimp, procuress
76 can transform/transmute beauty into its likeness
77 this was once something contrary to received opinion/belief
78 the current state of things shows that it has been proven
79 engraft a trunk/stem of a tree (or a human lineage/family line)
80 preserve traces of the "old stock," our original natures
81 more or less, tolerably
82 command
83 fellows (negative/low connotations) like me work at/be actively involved in
84 notorious/downright/unmitigated rogues

Hamlet   If thou dost marry, I'll give thee this plague for thy
dowry: be thou as chaste as ice, as pure as snow, thou shalt not   135
escape calumny.[85] Get thee to a nunnery, go: farewell. Or, if
thou wilt needs marry, marry a fool, for wise men know well
enough what monsters[86] you[87] make of them. To a nunnery,
go, and quickly too. Farewell.

Ophelia   O heavenly powers, restore him!   140

Hamlet   I have heard of your paintings[88] too, well enough. God
has given you one face, and you make yourselves another.
You jig, you amble, and you lisp,[89] and nickname God's
creatures,[90] and make your wantonness your ignorance.[91] Go
to,[92] I'll no more on't;[93] it hath made me mad. I say, we will   145
have no mo[94] marriage. Those that are married already – all
but one[95] – shall live. The rest shall keep[96] as they are. To a
nunnery, go.

EXIT HAMLET

Ophelia   O, what a noble mind is here o'erthrown!
The courtier's, soldier's, scholar's, eye – tongue – sword,   150

85 slander
86 cuckolds (because cuckolds were supposed to grow horns on their heads)
87 women in general (as in Hamlet's next speech)
88 cosmetic painting of a woman's face
89 you dance a lively, up-and-down dance, you dance in a smooth, easy
manner, you pretend to lisp (affectation of childlike nature)
90 another affectation
91 you pretend that your lewdness/unchastity is ignorance
92 come, come! (exclamation of disapproval)
93 I want no more to do with it
94 more
95 the king
96 remain

[handwritten annotation:] could be a scholar but doesn't have what he needs to be a scholar... tongue/ sword

Th' expectancy and rose of the fair state,[97]
The glass of fashion[98] and the mold of form,[99]
Th' observed of[100] all observers, quite, quite down![101]
And I, of ladies most deject and wretched,
155 That sucked the honey of his musicked[102] vows,
Now see that noble and most sovereign reason,[103]
Like sweet bells jangled, out of tune and harsh,
That unmatched form and feature of blown youth
Blasted with ecstasy.[104] O, woe is me,
160 T' have seen what I have seen, see what I see!

ENTER CLAUDIUS AND POLONIUS

Claudius Love? His affections do not that way tend,
Nor what he spake, though it lacked form a little,
Was not like madness. There's something in his soul,
O'er which his melancholy sits on brood,
165 And I do doubt the hatch and the disclose[105]
Will be some danger, which for to prevent
I have in quick determination
Thus set it down.[106] He shall with speed to England,[107]

---

97 the source of hope and the peerless/matchless person of an unblemished
  nation
98 mirror of behavior/demeanor
99 pattern/model of rank, quality, excellence, manners
100 he who was celebrated/respected by
101 descended, fallen
102 harmonious
103 most superlative mental power
104 that unmatched image of blossoming/flowering youth and comeliness
  blighted by madness
105 hatching, and I do fear/suspect that what will emerge from this hatching
106 authoritative decision decided (*and* written)
107 he must and will hurry to England

For the demand of our neglected tribute.[108]
Haply the seas and countries different,   170
With variable objects,[109] shall expel
This something-settled[110] matter in his heart,
Whereon[111] his brains still beating puts[112] him thus
From fashion of himself.[113] What think you on't?

Polonius It shall do well. But yet do I believe   175
The origin and commencement of his grief
Sprung from neglected love. (*to his daughter*) How now,
   Ophelia!
You need not tell us what Lord Hamlet said:
We heard it all. (*to the King*) My lord, do as you please,
But, if you hold it fit,[114] after the play   180
Let his queen mother all alone entreat him
To show his grief. Let her be round[115] with him;
And I'll be placed, so please you, in the ear[116]
Of all their conference. If she find him not,[117]
To England send him, or confine[118] him where   185
Your wisdom best shall think.

---

108 for the urgent/peremptory request of our disregarded/still unpaid tax/
   homage (the "Danegeld")
109 different countries and diverse material things
110 to some extent fixed/established
111 on which
112 always thrashing/dashing upon pushes, shoves
113 away from his normal behavior
114 think it proper/suitable
115 blunt, straightforward
116 within hearing
117 does not find out/learn about him
118 shut up, banish, imprison

Claudius   It shall be so:
Madness in great ones must not unwatched go.

EXEUNT

SCENE 2
The castle

ENTER HAMLET AND PLAYERS

Hamlet Speak the speech, I pray you, as I pronounced it to you,
trippingly[1] on the tongue. But if you mouth it[2] as many of
your players[3] do, I had as lief[4] the town-crier spoke my lines.
Nor do not saw[5] the air too much with your hand – thus –
but use all gently,[6] for in the very torrent, tempest, and – as I   5
may say – the whirlwind of passion, you must acquire and
beget a temperance that may give it smoothness.[7] O, it
offends me to the soul to hear a robustious periwig-pated
fellow[8] tear a passion to tatters, to very rags, to split the ears of
the groundlings,[9] who for the most part are capable of   10
nothing but inexplicable[10] dumbshows and noise.[11] I would

1 lightly, nimbly
2 declaim it, pompously / oratorically
3 players in general (that is, not necessarily speaking of these players)
4 as willingly
5 also do not gesticulate to and fro
6 perform everything like men of good breeding / birth / gentlemen
7 come to possess / get and generate / create a restraint / moderation that may
   give your words / speech smoothness
8 boisterous, wig-wearing fellow (negative / low connotation)
9 burst the ears of those in the cheap places, on the bare ground in front of the
   stage, without seating (implying less wealth and less education / learning)
10 nonverbal (and therefore unable to be explained in words)
11 acting without any words (in current usage, "mime-shows") and clamor /
    loud shouting

have such a fellow whipped for o'erdoing Termagant.[12] It
out-herods Herod.[13] Pray you, avoid it.

First Player I warrant[14] your honor.

15 *Hamlet* Be not too tame neither, but let your own discretion
be your tutor. Suit the action to the word, the word to the
action—with this special observance, that you o'erstep not
the modesty of nature.[15] For anything so o'erdone is from the
purpose of playing, whose end, both at the first and now,[16]
20 was and is, to hold, as 'twere, the mirror up to nature, to virtue
her own feature,[17] scorn[18] her own image, and the very age
and of the time his form and pressure.[19] Now this overdone,
or come off,[20] though it make the unskilful laugh cannot
but[21] make the judicious grieve – the censure of the which
25 one must in your allowance[22] o'erweigh a whole theater of
others. O, there be players that I have seen play, and heard
others praise, and that highly – not to speak it profanely[23] –

---

12 a violent character in the Mystery Plays, biblical folk-dramas popular in
England, thirteenth–sixteenth centuries
13 ruler of Galilee, who presided at the trial of Jesus: represented in the Mystery
Plays as almost hysterically violent
14 promise, guarantee
15 rule, do not transgress against the moderation of nature
16 aim/goal, both originally and now
17 shape, form
18 (a noun)
19 the age and essence/reality of the time itself its printed ("pressed-down-
on") stamp/image/character
20 come off sluggishly/sloppily
21 though it make the ignorant/unwise laugh, can only
22 the condemnation/critical disapproval of whom must in your balancing of
pro and con
23 to treat the sacred irreverently (that is, that God and only God created
humankind)

that, neither having th' accent of Christians nor the gait[24] of
Christian, pagan, nor man, have so strutted and bellowed that
I have thought some of nature's journeymen[25] had made   30
men, and not made them well, they imitated humanity so
abominably.

First Player I hope we have reformed that indifferently[26] with
us, sir.

Hamlet   O, reform it altogether. And let those that play your   35
clowns[27] speak no more than is set down for them, for there
be of them that will themselves laugh, to set on some quantity
of barren[28] spectators to laugh too, though, in the meantime,
some necessary question[29] of the play be then to be
considered. That's villanous,[30] and shows a most pitiful   40
ambition in the fool that uses it. Go, make you ready.

EXEUNT PLAYERS

ENTER POLONIUS, ROSENCRANTZ, AND GUILDENSTERN

(*to Polonius*) How now, my lord! Will the king hear this piece
of work?

Polonius   And the queen too, and that presently.

Hamlet   (*to Polonius*) Bid the players make haste.   45

EXIT POLONIUS

24 carriage, manner of walking
25 a worker out of his apprenticeship but not yet certified as a master craftsman
26 corrected/improved that to a considerable/tolerable degree
27 fools, jesters
28 dull
29 subject, matter
30 shameful, atrocious, detestable

Will you two help to hasten them?
Rosencrantz Ay, my lord.

EXEUNT ROSENCRANTZ AND GUILDENSTERN

Hamlet   What ho! Horatio!

ENTER HORATIO

Horatio   Here, sweet[31] lord, at your service.
50 *Hamlet*   Horatio, thou art e'en as just[32] a man
             As e'er my conversation coped withal.[33]
Horatio   O, my dear lord —
Hamlet   Nay, do not think I flatter,
             For what advancement[34] may I hope from thee
             That no revenue hast but thy good spirits,
55   To feed and clothe thee? Why should the poor be flattered?
             No, let the candied tongue lick absurd[35] pomp,
             And crook the pregnant[36] hinges of the knee
             Where thrift may follow fawning.[37] Dost thou hear?
             Since my dear soul was mistress of her choice
60   And could of men distinguish her election,[38]
             S'hath sealed[39] thee for herself, for thou hast been

31 dear
32 uniformly / regularly impartial / even-tempered
33 my experience in society / acquaintance has encountered / met with
34 promotion, preferment (political profit)
35 let the sugared / flattering / fawning / lying tongue lick ridiculous / silly
36 bend / bow the ready
37 there where prosperity / success may follow pretense of servile fondness (as a
   dog wags its tail)
38 make distinctions about her careful choice
39 she hath marked / decided on

As one, in suff'ring all, that suffers[40] nothing,
A man that Fortune's buffets[41] and rewards
Hast ta'en with equal thanks. And blest are those
Whose blood[42] and judgment are so well commeddled[43]   65
That they are not a pipe[44] for Fortune's finger
To sound[45] what stop she please. Give me that man
That is not passion's slave, and I will wear him
In my heart's core, ay, in my heart of heart,
As I do thee. — Something[46] too much of this.   70
There is a play to-night before the king.
One scene of it comes near[47] the circumstance
Which I have told thee, of my father's death.
I prithee, when thou seest that act afoot,[48]
Even with the very comment[49] of thy soul   75
Observe mine uncle. If his occulted[50] guilt
Do not itself unkennel[51] in one speech,
It is a damnèd ghost[52] that we have seen,

---

40 like one who, while experiencing/passing through everything, has been
    damaged/injured
41 blows
42 disposition, temper, mood, passion
43 commingled, mixed together
44 tube-like musical instrument made of reed or wood, blown on at one end,
    while the fingers cover and uncover holes ("stops") to produce variable
    pitches
45 blow, play
46 rather, a little
47 close to
48 performance/scene going on
49 true/reliable critical powers
50 hidden, secret
51 bring out into the light (literally, to come out of a lair, like a hunted animal)
52 a spirit from hell

And my imaginations are as foul[53]
80 As Vulcan's stithy.[54] Give him heedful[55] note,
For I mine eyes will rivet to his face,
And after we will both our judgments join
In censure of his seeming.[56]

Horatio   Well,[57] my lord.
If 'a steal aught the whilst this play is playing,
85 And 'scape detecting, I will pay the theft.

ENTER TRUMPETS AND KETTLEDRUMS

FLOURISH SOUNDS

Hamlet   They are coming to the play; I must be idle.[58]
Get you a place.

ENTER KING, QUEEN, POLONIUS, OPHELIA,
ROSENCRANTZ, GUILDENSTERN, LORDS ATTENDANT,
AND GUARDS CARRYING TORCHES

Claudius How fares[59] our cousin Hamlet?
Hamlet   Excellent, i' faith, of the chameleon's dish.[60] I eat the
90 air, promise-crammed. You cannot feed capons[61] so.
Claudius I have nothing with[62] this answer, Hamlet. These
words are not mine.

53 dirty, polluted
54 the god of metalworking's smithy/forge
55 careful/attentive/watchful notice
56 judgment/opinion (negative connotations) of his appearance
57 that's good/fine
58 frivolous, lightheaded
59 does (*or* eats)
60 air (which chameleons had long been thought to feed upon)
61 castrated cocks, crammed with food to make them better eating
62 I obtain, understand nothing by/from

Hamlet	No, nor mine now. (*to Polonius*) My lord, you
	played[63] once i' the university, you say?
Polonius	That did I, my lord, and was accounted a good actor. 95
Hamlet	What did you enact?
Polonius	I did enact Julius Caesar. I was killed i' the
	Capitol.[64] Brutus killed me.
Hamlet	It was a brute part of him to kill so capital[65] a calf
	there.—Be the players ready? 100
Rosencrantz	Ay, my lord. They stay upon your patience.[66]
Gertrude	Come hither, my dear Hamlet. Sit by me.
Hamlet	(*approaches Ophelia*) No, good mother. Here's metal
	more attractive.[67]
Polonius	(*to King*) O, ho! Do you mark that? 105
Hamlet	Lady, shall I lie in your lap?[68]

HE LIES AT OPHELIA'S FEET

Ophelia	No, my lord.
Hamlet	I mean, my head upon your lap?
Ophelia	Ay, my lord.
Hamlet	Do you think I meant country matters?[69] 110
Ophelia	I think nothing, my lord.
Hamlet	That's a fair thought to lie[70] between maids' legs.
Ophelia	What is, my lord?

63 acted
64 Roman temple, located on a hill
65 it was a cruel/coarse role/affair for him to kill so preeminent, important
66 wait for your leave/permission
67 magnetic
68 a clearly sexual allusion
69 rural/peasantlike matters (another sexual allusion, with a pun on "cunt")
70 put/place (with an unmistakable pun)

Hamlet   Nothing

115   *Ophelia*   You are merry,[71] my lord.

Hamlet   Who, I?

Ophelia   Ay, my lord.

Hamlet   O God, your only jig-maker.[72] What should a man do
but be merry? For look you how cheerfully my mother
120   looks, and my father died within's[73] two hours.

Ophelia   Nay, 'tis twice two months, my lord.

Hamlet   So long? Nay then, let the devil wear black,[74] for I'll
have a suit of sables.[75] O heavens! Die two months ago, and
not forgotten yet? Then there's hope a great man's memory
125   may outlive his life half a year. But by'r Lady, he must build
churches,[76] then, or else shall 'a suffer not[77] thinking on, with
the hobby-horse,[78] whose epitaph is "For O, for O,
the hobby-horse is forgot."

HAUTBOYS[79] PLAY. THE DUMB-SHOW[80] ENTERS

ENTER A KING AND A QUEEN VERY LOVINGLY, THE QUEEN
EMBRACING HIM, AND HE HER. SHE KNEELS, AND MAKES SHOW

---

71 pleasant, cheerful (with possibly a pun on "merry" = "tipsy")
72 the only composer of comic interludes
73 within this
74 the devil indeed wore black
75 black (though the soft, rich fur is dark brown; "black" is of course the color
of mourning clothes)
76 he (the dead man) must have financed/arranged for the building of
churches
77 not be permitted/allowed to be thought about
78 along with the hobby horse, a character in the traditional May games (and
also the morris dance), popularly thought of as likely to be forgotten; the
performer wore a wickerwork representation of a horse around the waist
79 oboes
80 mime

OF PROTESTATION[81] UNTO HIM. HE TAKES HER UP, AND
DECLINES[82] HIS HEAD UPON HER NECK. HE LIES HIM DOWN
UPON A BANK OF FLOWERS. SHE, SEEING HIM ASLEEP, LEAVES
HIM. ANON COMES IN A FELLOW, TAKES OFF HIS[83] CROWN,
KISSES IT, AND POURS POISON IN THE SLEEPER'S EARS, AND
EXITS. THE QUEEN RETURNS, FINDS THE KING DEAD, AND
MAKES PASSIONATE ACTION.[84] THE POISONER, WITH SOME
THREE OR FOUR,[85] COMES IN AGAIN. THEY SEEM TO
CONDOLE[86] WITH HER. THE DEAD BODY IS CARRIED AWAY. THE
POISONER WOOS THE QUEEN WITH GIFTS. SHE SEEMS HARSH[87]
AWHILE, BUT IN THE END ACCEPTS LOVE.

EXEUNT

Ophelia What means this, my lord?
Hamlet Marry, this is miching mallecho.[88] It means mischief.   130
Ophelia Belike this show imports the argument[89] of the play.

ENTER PROLOGUE[90]

Hamlet We shall know by this fellow The players cannot keep
counsel;[91] they'll tell all.
Ophelia Will 'a tell us what this show meant?

81 a solemn oath / request
82 helps / raises her up and lowers
83 the sleeping king's
84 strongly emotional motions / gestures
85 three or four men
86 grieve, lament, express sympathy
87 disinclined
88 skulking / sneaking mischief / misdeeds: MEECHing MALecko
89 perhaps / possibly this performance / spectacle introduces / expresses the
   theme / subject
90 an actor who delivers / speaks the prologue of the play
91 keep a secret, hold their tongues

135 *Hamlet*   Ay, or any show that you'll show him. Be not you
        ashamed to show, he'll not shame to tell you what it means.

    Ophelia   You are naught,[92] you are naught: I'll mark the play.

    Prologue   For us, and for our tragedy,
        Here stooping[93] to your clemency,
140   We beg your hearing patiently.

EXIT

    Hamlet   Is this a prologue, or the posy of[94] a ring?
    Ophelia   'Tis brief, my lord.
    Hamlet   As woman's love.

ENTER TWO PLAYERS, KING AND QUEEN

    Player King   Full thirty times hath Phoebus' cart[95] gone round
145   Neptune's salt wash and Tellus' orbèd ground,[96]
    And thirty dozen moons with borrowed sheen[97]
    About the world have times twelve thirties[98] been,
    Since love our hearts, and Hymen[99] did our hands,
    Unite commutual in most sacred bands.[100]
150 *Player Queen*   So many journeys may the sun and moon
    Make us again count o'er ere love be done!
    But woe is me, you are so sick of late,

92 wicked, naughty
93 bowing, submitting
94 inscription on
95 the sun's chariot
96 the sea god's salt waves/water and the earth god's rounded lands
97 gleam, radiance
98 "times twelve thirties" = "twelve times thirty" (360 months = 30 years)
99 Greek god of marriage
100 mutually, reciprocally in most sacred bonds

So far from cheer and from your former state,
That I distrust you.[101] Yet though I distrust,
Discomfort you, my lord, it nothing must,[102]   155
For women fear too much, even as they love,
And women's fear and love hold quantity[103]
In neither aught, or in extremity.[104]
Now, what my love is, proof hath made you know;
And as my love is sized, my fear is so.[105]   160
Where love is great, the littlest doubts are fear;
Where little fears grow great, great love grows there.

Player King   'Faith, I must leave thee, love, and shortly too;
My operant powers their functions leave to do,[106]
And thou shalt live in this fair world behind,[107]   165
Honored, beloved – and haply one as kind
For husband shalt tho –

Player Queen O, confound[108] the rest!
Such love must needs be treason in my breast.
In second husband let me be accurst!   170
None wed the second but who killed the first.

Hamlet   (*aside*) That's wormwood.[109]

Player Queen The instances that second marriage move[110]

101 doubt you, worry about you
102 the fact that *she* worries ought not to worry *him* ("discomfort":"sadden,
    deprive of comfort")
103 preserve/keep proportion (to each other)
104 neither in little things nor in large ones
105 just as my love is large, my fear is the same
106 my vital forces stop their work
107 after me
108 to hell with
109 bitter/unpleasant (wormwood: a singularly bitter herb)
110 causes/motives that second marriage originate

Are base respects of thrift,[111] but none of love:
175 A second time I kill my husband dead
When second husband kisses me in bed.
Player King I do believe you think what now you speak,
But what we do determine oft we break.[112]
Purpose is but the slave to memory,
180 Of violent birth, but poor validity;[113]
Which now, like fruit unripe, sticks on the tree,
But fall, unshaken, when they mellow[114] be.
Most necessary 'tis that we forget
To pay ourselves what to ourselves is debt.
185 What to ourselves in passion we propose,
The passion ending, doth the purpose lose.
The violence[115] of either grief or joy
Their own enactures with themselves[116] destroy:
Where joy most revels,[117] grief doth most lament:
190 Grief joys, joy grieves, on slender accident.[118]
This world is not for aye,[119] nor 'tis not strange
That even our loves should with our fortunes change,
For 'tis a question left us yet to prove,
Whether love lead[120] fortune, or else fortune[121] love.

111 shabby/degrading/selfish considerations of an economic nature
112 decide upon/resolve often we fail to act upon
113 of vivid/intense birth, but poor soundness
114 ripe, mature
115 VIoLENCE
116 performance/actuation with their own violence/extreme natures
117 takes pleasure, enjoys itself, makes merry
118 slight/trifling chance/fortune
119 ever
120 shows the way for, guides
121 fortune leads

The great man down, you mark his favorite flies;[122]   195
The poor advanced[123] makes friends of enemies.
And hitherto[124] doth love on fortune tend,[125]
For who not needs shall never lack a friend,
And who in want a hollow friend doth try[126]
Directly seasons[127] him his enemy.   200
But orderly[128] to end where I begun,
Our wills and fates do so contrary[129] run
That our devices[130] still are overthrown:
Our thoughts are ours, their ends none of our own.
So think thou wilt no second husband wed,   205
But die[131] thy thoughts when thy first lord[132] is dead.

Player Queen Nor earth to me give food, nor heaven light,
Sport and repose lock from me day and night –
To desperation turn my trust and hope,
An anchor's[133] cheer in prison be my scope[134] –   210
Each opposite that blanks the face of joy
Meet what I would have well, and it destroy[135] –

122 the person on whom he has showered regard and favors flees
123 the poor man raised up/promoted
124 thus far (in the long history of humanity)
125 attend, wait upon
126 an insincere friend puts to the proof
127 ripens, matures
128 in a disciplined/well-conducted manner
129 conTRAry
130 purposes, intentions
131 expire, perish
132 husband
133 anchorite/hermit's fare/food/entertainment
134 goal, desired end
135 may each adverse force that turns pale the face of joy have an encounter
     with what I want, and destroy it

Both here and hence[136] pursue me lasting strife –
If once a widow, ever I be wife!

215 *Hamlet*   If she should break it[137] now!

Player King   'Tis deeply sworn. Sweet, leave me here awhile.
My spirits grow dull, and fain I would beguile
The tedious day with sleep.[138]

HE SLEEPS

Player Queen   Sleep rock thy brain,[139]
And never come mischance between us twain![140]

EXIT

220 *Hamlet*   (*to Gertrude*) Madam, how like you this play?

Gertrude   The lady doth protest too much, methinks.

Hamlet   O, but she'll keep her word.

Claudius   Have you heard the argument?[141] Is there no
offence in 't?

225 *Hamlet*   No, no, they do but jest, poison in jest – no
offence i' the world.

Claudius   What do you[142] call the play?

Hamlet   "The Mouse-trap." Marry, how? Tropically.[143] This
play is the image[144] of a murder done in Vienna. Gonzago is

---

136 here on earth (in this life) and afterward (in life eternal)
137 her vow
138 listless/depressed, and I want to turn the wearisome day in a more
pleasant/cheerful direction by sleeping
139 sleep soothe thy brain (as a child is soothed by being rocked)
140 bad luck, disaster between the two of us
141 the contents/story
142 what's the play called
143 metaphorically
144 copy, likeness, imitation

the duke's name; his wife, Baptista. You shall see anon. 'Tis a   230
knavish piece of work – but what o' that? Your Majesty, and
we that have free[145] souls, it touches us not. Let the galled
jade wince:[146] our withers[147] are unwrung.[148]

ENTER LUCIANUS

This is one Lucianus, nephew to the King.

Ophelia You are as good as a chorus,[149] my lord.   235

Hamlet I could interpret[150] between you and your love, if I
could see the puppets dallying.[151]

Ophelia You are keen,[152] my lord, you are keen.

Hamlet It would cost you a groaning to take off my edge.[153]

Ophelia Still better,[154] and worse.[155]   240

Hamlet So you mistake[156] your husbands. (*to Player*) Begin,
murderer. Leave thy damnable faces,[157] and begin. Come: the
croaking raven doth bellow for revenge.

Lucianus Thoughts black, hands apt, drugs fit, and time
agreeing,[158]

---

145 honorable, innocent
146 let a chafed (made sore by harness/saddle rubbing), worn-out, worthless
    horse wince (in current usage, "if the shoe fits – and on us it doesn't –
    wear it")
147 high on a horse's back, between the shoulder blades
148 not hurt/wracked
149 an onstage performer who explains and annotates a play's action
150 supply the dialogue (as does a puppeteer, speaking on behalf of his puppets)
151 sporting (in current usage, "making out")
152 (1) sharp, bitter, (2) sexually aroused
153 at the loss of her virginity, to ease off/remove his sharpness/sexual desire
154 as a witticism
155 as a personal/social comment
156 miss take ("take in error")
157 leave off/stop making your horrible/worthy of damnation faces
158 appropriate, suitable/harmonious

245   Confederate season, else no creature seeing:[159]
       Thou mixture rank, of[160] midnight weeds collected,
       With Hecate's[161] ban thrice blasted, thrice infected,[162]
       Thy natural magic and dire property[163]
       On wholesome life usurp immediately.[164]

HE POURS POISON INTO THE SLEEPER'S EARS

250 *Hamlet*   He poisons him i' the garden for's estate.[165] His[166] name's Gonzago. The story is extant, and written in very choice[167] Italian. You shall see anon how the murderer gets the love of Gonzago's wife.

    Ophelia   The king rises.

255 *Hamlet*   What, frighted with false fire?[168]

    Gertrude   How fares my lord?

    Polonius   Give o'er[169] the play.

    Claudius   Give me some light. Away!

    Polonius   Lights, lights, lights!

EXEUNT ALL BUT HAMLET AND HORATIO

---

159 cooperative time / occasion, no other creature seeing
160 coarse / loathsome / violent, from
161 deity of ghosts and magic (properly pronounced HECaTEE, the name is here pronounced HEcate)
162 curse three times blighted / balefully affected, three times imbued / saturated / impregnated
163 innate magic and dreadful / terrible characteristic / nature
164 take immediate control / seize possession of healthy life
165 for his rank, fortune
166 the King's
167 fine, excellent
168 blank bullets
169 leave off, finish, stop

Hamlet Why, let the strucken[170] deer go weep, 260
    The hart ungallèd[171] play,
For some must watch, while some must sleep:
    So runs the world away.

Would not this, sir, and a forest of feathers[172] – if the rest of
my fortunes Turk[173] with me – with two Provincial roses on 265
my razed[174] shoes, get me a fellowship in a cry of players?[175]
Horatio Half a share.
Hamlet A whole one, I.[176]

For thou dost know, O Damon[177] dear,
    This realm dismantled was 270
Of Jove himself,[178] and now reigns here
    A very, very – pajock.[179]
Horatio You might have rhymed.[180]
Hamlet O good Horatio, I'll take[181] the ghost's word for a
thousand pound. Didst perceive? 275
Horatio Very well, my lord.

170 wounded
171 undistressed stag
172 actors' costumes included befeathered hats
173 change completely (the basis of the phrase is conversion from Christianity
    to Islam)
174 roses from Provence on my shoes, decorated with slashes
175 a partnership (as a playwright) in a pack of actors
176 say I
177 Hamlet is not being capricious: Damon and Pythias were proverbial friends
    in ancient Greece
178 of Hamlet's Jove-like father
179 peacock
180 the comment is not aimed not at Hamlet's poetic abilities but at the King:
    the predictable rhyme for "was" – and Hamlet visibly delays, at this point –
    would have been "ass"
181 accept a bet on

Hamlet	Upon[182] the talk of the poisoning?
Horatio	I did very well note him.
Hamlet	Ah, ha! Come, some music! Come, the recorders![183]

280   For if the king like not the comedy,
Why then, belike[184] he likes it not, perdy.[185]

Come, some music!

ENTER ROSENCRANTZ AND GUILDENSTERN

Guildenstern	Good my lord, vouchsafe[186] me a word with you.
Hamlet	Sir, a whole history.
285 *Guildenstern*	The king, sir –
Hamlet	Ay, sir, what of[187] him?
Guildenstern	Is in his retirement[188] marvellous distempered.[189]
Hamlet	With drink, sir?
Guildenstern	No, my lord, rather with choler.[190]
290 *Hamlet*	Your wisdom should show itself more richer to signify[191] this to his doctor – for, for me to put him to his purgation[192] would perhaps plunge him into far more choler.

182 right after
183 wooden flutes played in a vertical position (modern flutes are made of metal and played transversely)
184 probably
185 by God (*par dieu*)
186 grant
187 about
188 withdrawal from this public location
189 astonishingly disordered/out of temper
190 anger
191 better/of more worth, to communicate
192 "choler" can mean (though here it obviously does not) an excess of bile ("biliousness"), which was treated by use of a cathartic; purgation: emptying the bowels

Guildenstern Good my lord, put your discourse into some frame and start[193] not so wildly from my affair.[194]

Hamlet I am tame,[195] sir. Pronounce.[196]   295

Guildenstern The queen, your mother, in most great affliction of spirit, hath sent me to you.

Hamlet You are welcome.

Guildenstern Nay, good my lord, this courtesy is not of the right breed.[197] If it shall please you to make me a wholesome[198]   300
answer, I will do your mother's commandment. If not, your pardon[199] and my return shall be the end of my business.

Hamlet Sir, I cannot.

Rosencrantz What, my lord?

Hamlet Make you a wholesome answer. My wit's diseased.   305
But, sir, such answer as I can make, you shall command – or, rather, as you say, my mother. Therefore no more, but to the matter. My mother, you say –

Rosencrantz Then thus she says: your behavior hath struck her into amazement and admiration.[200]   310

Hamlet O wonderful son, that can so stonish[201] a mother! But is there no sequel at the heels of this mother's admiration? Impart.[202]

193 order/logic and do not leap/jump
194 business
195 under control
196 speak
197 strain, species
198 sound
199 permission to leave
200 wonder
201 O son full of wonder, who can so astonish
202 communicate

Rosencrantz She desires to speak with you in her closet,[203] ere
315 you go to bed.

Hamlet   We shall obey, were she ten times our mother.[204]
Have you any further trade[205] with us?

Rosencrantz My lord, you once did love me.

Hamlet   So I do still, by these pickers and stealers.[206]

320 *Rosencrantz* Good my lord, what is your cause of distemper?[207]
You do surely bar the door upon your own liberty, if you
deny[208] your griefs to your friend.

Hamlet   Sir, I lack advancement.[209]

Rosencrantz How can that be, when you have the voice of the
325 King himself for your succession[210] in Denmark?

Hamlet   Ay, but sir, "While the grass grows"[211] – the
proverb is something musty.[212]

ENTER PLAYERS WITH RECORDERS

O, the recorders! Let me see one. (*to Rosencrantz*) To
withdraw[213] with you – why do you go about to recover the

203 private room
204 a quixotic observation that no one appears to quite understand
205 commerce, dealings (an insult: someone who is "in trade" is of inferior
social status)
206 hands: the catechism in the Anglican Book of Common Prayer warns,
"keep my hands from picking and stealing"
207 mental disorder, derangement
208 refuse to admit/acknowledge
209 progress in status, upward movement, promotion
210 expressed will/choice of the King himself for your succession to the
throne
211 while the grass grows, the horse starves
212 a bit antiquated/stale
213 to be intimate/private

wind of me, as if you would drive me into a toil?[214]   330

Guildenstern O, my lord, if my duty be too bold,[215] my love is
too unmannerly.[216]

Hamlet   I do not well understand that. Will you play upon
this pipe?

Guildenstern My lord, I cannot.   335

Hamlet   I pray you.

Guildenstern Believe me, I cannot.

Hamlet   I do beseech you.

Guildenstern I know no touch of it,[217] my lord.

Hamlet   'Tis as easy as lying. Govern these ventages[218] with   340
your fingers and thumb, give it breath with your mouth, and
it will discourse[219] most eloquent music. Look you, these are
the stops.

Guildenstern But these cannot I command to any utterance of
harmony.[220] I have not the skill.   345

Hamlet   Why, look you now, how unworthy a thing you
make of me! You would play upon me; you would seem to
know my stops; you would pluck out the heart of my
mystery;[221] you would sound[222] me from my lowest note to

214 to get upwind of me (from hunting: smelling a person upwind of it, the
     hunted animal runs in the other direction, right into the "toil," a net or nets
     placed for capture)
215 actions/words be too daring/presumptuous
216 my love makes me rude/discourteous/wanting in good manners
217 I do not know how to touch/play on it
218 manage/work these finger holes/stops
219 utter
220 control, master to any harmonious/pleasing/agreeable effect
221 secrets
222 measure, plumb, examine

350 the top of my compass[223] – and there is much music,
excellent voice, in this little organ,[224] yet cannot you make it
speak. 'Sblood, do you think I am easier to be played on than
a pipe? Call me what instrument you will, though you can
fret[225] me, yet you cannot play upon me.

ENTER POLONIUS

355 God bless you, sir!

Polonius My lord, the Queen would speak with you, and
presently.

Hamlet Do you see yonder cloud that's almost in shape of a
camel?

360 *Polonius* By the mass, and 'tis like a camel, indeed.

Hamlet Methinks it is like a weasel.

Polonius It is backed like[226] a weasel.

Hamlet Or like a whale.

Polonius Very like a whale.

365 *Hamlet* Then I will come to my mother by and by.[227] (*aside*)
They fool me to the top of my bent.[228] (*to Polonius*) I will
come by and by.

Polonius I will say so.

Hamlet "By and by" is easily said.

EXIT POLONIUS

370 Leave me, friends.

---

223 range of musical tones
224 sounds/musical capacity in this little musical instrument
225 (1) distress, gnaw at, (2) put fret bars on (like a guitar)
226 forms a back similar to
227 soon, right away
228 make a fool of/dupe me to the fullest degree of tension in my bow

EXEUNT ALL BUT HAMLET

'Tis now the very witching time of night,
When churchyards yawn[229] and hell itself breathes out
Contagion[230] to this world. Now could I drink hot blood
And do such bitter[231] business as the day
Would quake to look on. Soft! Now to my mother.   375
O heart, lose not thy nature. Let not ever
The soul of Nero[232] enter this firm[233] bosom.
Let me be cruel, not unnatural.
I will speak daggers to her, but use none.
My tongue and soul in this be hypocrites.[234]   380
How in my words somever she be shent,[235]
To give them seals[236]—never, my soul, consent!

EXIT

229 gape open
230 moral pestilence/plague/poison
231 painful, cruel, virulent
232 emperor of Rome, who murdered his mother, Agrippina
233 constant, steadfast
234 must be dissemblers/pretenders
235 howsoever she be disgraced in what I say
236 carry words into effect,/transform them into deeds (as seals legitimate and
   complete written documents)

SCENE 3
The castle

ENTER CLAUDIUS, ROSENCRANTZ, AND GUILDENSTERN

Claudius   I like him not, nor stands it safe with us[1]
To let his madness range.[2] Therefore prepare you.
I your commission will forthwith dispatch,[3]
And he to England shall along with you.
5   The terms of our estate[4] may not endure
Hazard so near us as doth hourly grow
Out of his brows.

Guildenstern   We will ourselves provide.[5]
Most holy and religious[6] fear it is
To keep those many many bodies safe
10   That live and feed upon[7] your majesty.

Rosencrantz   The single[8] and peculiar life is bound,
With all the strength and armor of the mind,
To keep itself from noyance,[9] but much more
That spirit upon whose weal[10] depends and rests
15   The lives of many. The cess[11] of majesty
Dies not alone; but, like a gulf[12] doth draw

---

1 I do not approve of him, nor does it remain safe for me
2 roam at large, extend itself
3 complete immediately
4 the circumstances of my rank/place
5 prepare/ready ourselves
6 pious/conscientious
7 by reliance on
8 individual
9 vexation, molestation ("annoyance")
10 welfare, well-being
11 cessation (death)
12 whirlpool

What's near it with it. It is a massy wheel,
Fixed on the summit of the highest mount,
To whose huge spokes ten thousand lesser things
Are mortised and adjoined,[13] which when it falls,   20
Each small annexment (petty consequence!)
Attends the boist'rous[14] ruin. Never alone
Did the king sigh, but with a general[15] groan.
Claudius Arm[16] you, I pray you, to this speedy voyage,
For we will fetters[17] put upon this fear,   25
Which now goes too free-footed.
Rosencrantz, Guildenstern   We will haste us.

ᴇxᴇᴜɴᴛ Rosᴇɴᴄʀᴀɴᴛᴢ ᴀɴᴅ Gᴜɪʟᴅᴇɴsᴛᴇʀɴ

ᴇɴᴛᴇʀ Pᴏʟᴏɴɪᴜs

Polonius My lord, he's going to his mother's closet.
Behind the arras I'll convey myself
To hear the process.[18] I'll warrant she'll tax him home,[19]
And as you said — and wisely was it said —   30
'Tis meet that some more audience than a mother
(Since nature makes them partial) should o'erhear
The speech, of vantage.[20] Fare you well, my liege.
I'll call upon you ere you go to bed,

---

13 fastened/secured and united
14 adjunct/accessory of small, trivial/minor importance/little weight
   accompanies the painfully rough
15 universal
16 prepare yourselves for
17 chains, shackles
18 behind the hanging tapestry screen I'll place myself to hear what goes on
19 guarantee/predict she'll censure/reprove him pointedly/effectively/
   directly
20 from an advantageous location

And tell you what I know.

35 *Claudius*   Thanks, dear my lord.

EXIT POLONIUS

O, my offence is rank,[21] it smells to heaven,
It hath the primal eldest curse[22] upon't,
A brother's murder. Pray can I not,
Though inclination be as sharp[23] as will.

40 My stronger guilt defeats my strong intent,
And like a man to double[24] business bound
I stand in pause[25] where I shall first begin,
And both neglect. What if this cursèd hand
Were thicker than itself with brother's blood,

45 Is there not rain enough in the sweet heavens
To wash it white as snow? Whereto serves mercy[26]
But to confront the visage of offence?[27]
And what's in prayer but this two-fold force,
To be forestalled[28] ere we come to fall,

50 Or pardoned being down?[29] Then I'll look up,
My fault is past. But O, what form of prayer
Can serve my turn?[30] "Forgive me my foul murder?"

action
forgive him for his sin.
Keep him from going to hell
fault: murder: not admitting of being guilty
guilt of marrying his sister-in-law

21 gross, excessive, exceedingly great
22 Cain's murder of his brother, Abel
23 disposition/propensity/liking be as keen/eager/intense
24 deceitful, two-faced
25 ready/embarking on I stand in hesitation
26 what use is mercy
27 but to stand up to/defy the face/appearance of sin, wrong
28 for us to be prevented/stopped
29 or to be pardoned having fallen
30 purpose

That cannot be, since I am still possessed
Of those effects[31] for which I did the murder,
My crown, mine own ambition, and my queen.   55
May one be pardoned and retain th' offence?
In the corrupted currents[32] of this world
Offence's gilded hand may shove by[33] justice,
And oft 'tis seen the wicked prize[34] itself
Buys out the law. But 'tis not so above.   60
There is no shuffling,[35] there the action lies
In his[36] true nature, and we ourselves compelled,
Even to the teeth and forehead of our faults,[37]
To give in[38] evidence. What then? what rests?[39]
Try what repentance can:[40] what can it not?   65
Yet what can it when one can not repent?
O wretched state! O bosom[41] black as death!
O limèd[42] soul, that, struggling to be free,
Art more engaged![43] Help, angels! Make assay![44]
Bow, stubborn knees; and, heart with strings[45] of steel,   70

31 contemplated results/purposes
32 course of events
33 hand covered with gold may shove to the side/away
34 reward
35 there, there is no trickery/evasion
36 the act/deed is spread out in its
37 even confronting, face to face, our sins
38 deliver, hand in
39 remains
40 can do
41 not the physical chest, but the thoughts harbored inside: in the heart
42 trapped/snared (as birdlime spread on branches catches birds)
43 entangled
44 try
45 sinews, fibers

Be soft as sinews of the newborn babe!
All may be well.

RETIRES AND KNEELS

ENTER HAMLET

Hamlet Now might I do it pat,[46] now he is praying;
And now I'll do't. (*draws his sword*) And so[47] 'a goes to heaven;

75   And so am I revenged. That would be scanned.[48]
A villain kills my father; and for that,
I, his sole son, do this same villain send
To heaven.
O, this is hire and salary,[49] not revenge.

80   'A took my father grossly, full of bread,[50]
With all his crimes broad blown, as flush as May;[51]
And how his audit stands who knows save heaven?
But in our circumstance and course of thought,[52]
'Tis heavy with[53] him. And am I then revenged,

85   To take him in the purging of his soul,[54]
When he is fit and seasoned for his passage?[55]
No!

46 readily, conveniently
47 thus
48 that needs to be examined/considered
49 being hired to do a job, and then being paid for it
50 took my father indecently, in the midst of life's sensual indulgences
51 his sins plainly/amply/emphatically in bloom
52 our earthly condition and usual/customary way of thinking
53 serious, gloomy
54 to catch him in the midst of cleansing/purifying his soul
55 ready and prepared/ripened for the transition from this world to the next

Up, sword,[56] and know thou a more horrid hent.[57]
(*he sheathes his sword*) When he is drunk asleep, or in his rage,
Or in th'incestuous pleasure of his bed;   90
At gaming, a-swearing, or about some act
That has no relish[58] of salvation in't;
Then trip him, that his heels may kick at heaven,[59] *image*
And that his soul may be as damned and black
As hell, whereto it goes. My mother stays:[60]   95
This physic but prolongs thy sickly days.

EXIT

Claudius (*rising*) My words fly up, my thoughts remain below:
Words without thoughts never to heaven go.

EXIT.

*Can't always have things
you'r way
•nothing is perfect*

56 back in your sheathe, sword
57 plan
58 trace, tinge, flavor
59 so he is facing in the proper direction, which for him is toward hell
60 waits

SCENE 4

The queen's closet

ENTER GERTRUDE AND POLONIUS

Polonius 'A will come straight. Look you lay home to him.
Tell him his pranks have been too broad to bear with,
And that your grace hath screened[1] and stood between
Much heat[2] and him. I'll silence me even here.[3]
5 Pray you, be round with him.
Hamlet (*within*) Mother, mother, mother!
Gertrude I'll warrant you. Fear me not. Withdraw, I hear him
coming.

POLONIUS HIDES BEHIND THE ARRAS

ENTER HAMLET

Hamlet Now, mother, what's the matter?
Gertrude Hamlet, thou hast thy father[4] much offended.[5]
10 *Hamlet* Mother, you have my father[6] much offended.
Gertrude Come, come, you answer with an idle[7] tongue.
Hamlet Go, go, you question with a wicked tongue.
Gertrude Why, how now,[8] Hamlet!
Hamlet   What's the matter now?

---

1 protected, sheltered
2 anger
3 be still/silent exactly/precisely here
4 the King
5 sinned against/wronged (*and/or* displeased/angered/pained)
6 the deceased king
7 frivolous, trifling
8 what's this

Gertrude Have you forgot me?[9]
Hamlet   No, by the rood,[10] not so!
　You are the queen, your husband's brother's wife;   15
　And – would it were not so – you are my mother.
Gertrude Nay, then, I'll set those to you that can speak.[11]
Hamlet   Come, come, and sit you down. You shall not budge.

(HE PREVENTS HER FROM RISING)

　You go not till I set you up a glass[12]
　Where you may see the inmost part of you.   20
Gertrude What wilt thou do? thou wilt not murder me?
　Help, ho!
Polonius (*behind the arras*) What, ho! Help, help, help!
Hamlet   (*drawing his sword*) How now! A rat?[13] Dead for a
　ducat,[14] dead!

(HE THRUSTS HIS SWORD THROUGH THE ARRAS)

Polonius (*behind*) O, I am slain!
Gertrude   O me, what hast thou done?   25
Hamlet   Nay, I know not. Is it the king?
Gertrude O, what a rash and bloody deed is this!
Hamlet   A bloody deed? Almost as bad, good mother,
　As kill a king, and marry with his brother.

9 forgotten who I am
10 the crucifix, the true cross
11 I'll have you dealt with by those in authority
12 mirror
13 (perhaps referring to the noises rats made, attracting men to seek them out
　and kill them)
14 I'll kill whoever it is, for the price of a ducat (or "I'll bet a ducat this kills
　whoever it is")

Gertrude As kill a king!

30 *Hamlet*   Ay, lady, 'twas my word.

(LIFTS UP THE ARRAY AND REVEALS POLONIUS, DEAD)

Thou wretched, rash, intruding fool, farewell!
I took thee for thy better. Take thy fortune.[15]
Thou find'st to be too busy is some danger.[16]
(*to his mother*) Leave[17] wringing of your hands. Peace![18] Sit
you down
35 And let me wring your heart, for so I shall,
If it be made of penetrable stuff,
If damnèd custom have not brazed[19] it so
That it be proof and bulwark against sense.[20]

Gertrude What have I done, that thou dar'st wag thy tongue
In noise so rude against me?

40 *Hamlet*   Such an act
That blurs the grace and blush of modesty,[21]
Calls[22] virtue hypocrite, takes off the rose[23]
From the fair forehead of an innocent love
And sets a blister[24] there, makes marriage-vows

---

15 accept your luck
16 you've discovered/learned that to be prying/meddlesome/officious
involves/carries with it a degree of risk
17 stop
18 be still/silent
19 habit has not hardened it (like brass)
20 of tested and experienced strength (like armor) and a fortification against
emotion/feeling
21 stains/disfigures/befouls the attractive/becoming quality and glow of
proper womanly behavior
22 proclaims
23 beauty, fragrance (a sign of pure and virtuous love)
24 brand (prostitutes were branded on the forehead)

As false as dicers' oaths.[25] O, such a deed   45
As from the body of contraction[26] plucks
The very soul, and sweet religion makes
A rhapsody[27] of words. Heaven's face doth glow
O'er this solidity and compound mass[28]
With tristful visage,[29] as against the doom,[30]   50
Is thought-sick[31] at the act.

Gertrude   Ay me, what act,
That roars so loud, and thunders in the index?[32]

Hamlet   (*producing pictures*) Look here, upon this picture, and on
this,
The counterfeit presentment of two brothers.[33]
See what a grace was seated on this brow: 55
Hyperion's[34] curls, the front[35] of Jove himself,
An eye like Mars, to threaten and command;
A station[36] like the herald Mercury[37]
New-lighted on a heaven-kissing[38] hill –

[Handwritten annotations: GODS R / The picture 55 / of health / which contrasts / the fungus]

[Handwritten annotation: ✳ Character Development of / the king & Claudius]

25 gamblers' vows/promises
26 marriage (which is a contract)
27 is turned/transformed into a confused mass/an exalted expression without
   rational, connected thought
28 this solid and composite mass (that is, the earth)
29 with sad/sorrowful face/features
30 as it would be if in full view of/facing the day of judgment
31 *compare* heart-sick or soul-sick
32 this prologue (of yours) (*compare* the pointing index finger, scanning down a
   listing/a table of contents)
33 imitated/copied image/likeness of two brothers: Hamlet's father and his
   father's brother, the King
34 Hyperion: a Titan, father of Helios, the sun god
35 face
36 stance, way/manner of standing
37 messenger/herald of the gods
38 newly alighted on a hill so very high that it touches the skies/heaven

[Handwritten annotation: The king was a godly figure. / Claudius lives off the king like a / fungus]

Handwritten annotations (top): Ears, Eyes & Senses / lost her sense of reality / *Imagery! Repitions of the Eyes & Ears*

60   A combination and a form[39] indeed
      Where every god did seem to set his seal,
      To give the world assurance of a man.
      This *was* your husband. Look you now what follows.
      Here *is* your husband, like a mildewed[40] ear,
65   Blasting his wholesome[41] brother. Have you eyes?
      Could you on this fair mountain leave to feed
      And batten on this moor?[42] Ha! Have you eyes?
      You cannot call it love, for at your age
      The hey-day[43] in the blood is tame, it's humble
70   And waits upon[44] the judgment, and what judgment
      Would step from this to this? Sense sure[45] you have,
      Else could you not have motion,[46] but sure that sense
      Is apoplexed,[47] for madness would not err,[48]
      Nor sense to ecstasy was ne'er so thralled
75   But it reserved some quantity of choice[49]
      To serve in such a difference.[50] What devil was't
      That thus hath cozened you at hoodman-blind?[51]

Handwritten annotations (right margin): blind & deaf / loss of feelin / no heart / Rotten fruit / could also be refering to the rotting of the fruit of the loom / like all offspring are to be evil or corrupt like the parents / Stronger sound dialogue / Mild > the pharaoh was scared of dieing of a mildewed ear*

39 shape, body
40 fungus-ridden
41 blighting (like an infectious disease) his healthy brtoher
42 give over/stop feeding and glut yourself on this waste ground/marsh
43 time of life with the highest level of excitement
44 of lowered urgency and waits for/defers to/serves
45 reliable perceptive faculties
46 be able to move
47 arrested, interfered with (an affliction believed to be caused by a sudden flow of blood to the brain)
48 go astray/wrong (that is, you cannot be mad, because this is not the sort of error that madness makes)
49 nor were the faculties of perception ever so enslaved by the raptures of passion that sense did not retain a certain amount of choice
50 to assist in such a dispute/quarrel
51 cheated/defrauded you at blindman's buff

how can she not see what he sees.

*Relationships: Hamlet's relationship between his mother, him comes out in this scene. Hamlet shows his disgust with his mother.

Eyes without feeling, feeling without sight,
Ears without hands or eyes, smelling sans all,[52]
Or but a sickly part of one true sense,[53]   80
Could not so mope.[54]
O shame, where is thy blush? Rebellious hell,
If thou canst mutine[55] in a matron's bones,
To flaming youth let virtue be as wax
And melt in her own fire. Proclaim no shame   85
When the compulsive ardor gives the charge,[56]
Since frost itself as actively doth burn[57]
And reason panders will.[58]

Gertrude   O Hamlet, speak no more.
Thou turn'st mine eyes into[59] my very soul,
And there I see such black and grainèd spots[60]   90
As will not leave their tinct.[61]

Hamlet   Nay, but to live
In the rank sweat of an enseamèd bed,
Stewed in corruption,[62] honeying and making love

52 without everything
53 even just a feeble/weak/unhealthy portion of real/genuine/honest sense
54 could not be so aimless/spiritless
55 incite to revolt, rebel, mutiny
56 the enforced/coercive heat of passion/desire signals/sounds the impetuous
    attack
57 even the frigidity/coldness (of a "matron" like Gertrude) burns just as
    actively
58 reason serves as a pimp/pander for emotion/will
59 "into" expresses a direction, rather than a destination: Gertrude's vision has
    been redirected to look inward
60 the blemishes created by grain-produced dyes (colorfast and very durable)
61 which will not give up/lose their hue/color
62 greasy bed, steeped, overheated ("stew" = "whore"; "the stews" = "whore-
    houses")

Theme: Lust vs. Love

⌊ Over the nasty sty⁶³ ⌋

Gertrude   O, speak to me no more.
95   These words like daggers enter in mine ears.
      No more, sweet Hamlet!
Hamlet   A murderer and a villain,
      A slave that is not twentieth part the tithe
      Of your precedent lord⁶⁴ – a Vice⁶⁵ of kings,
      A cutpurse of the empire and the rule,⁶⁶
100   That from a shelf the precious diadem⁶⁷ stole
      And put it in his pocket –
Gertrude   No more!
Hamlet   A king of shreds and patches⁶⁸ –

ENTER GHOST

      Save me, and hover o'er me with your wings,
      You heavenly guards! What would your gracious figure?⁶⁹
105 Gertrude   Alas, he's mad!
Hamlet   Do you not come your tardy son to chide,
      That, lapsed in time and passion, lets go by⁷⁰
      Th' important acting⁷¹ of your dread command?
      O, say!

63 sweet-talking and making love over the foul/filthy place of bestial lust, a
   whorehouse
64 a rascal/fellow who is not a twentieth of a tenth (an exceedingly small
   percentage) of your prior husband
65 Vice was a villainous clown in the Morality Plays
66 a pickpocket/thief of the kingdom and the kingship
67 crown
68 of fragments/bits and pieces and botched-up/clumsy repairs
69 form, shape
70 son to scold, who, fallen away both in time and in passion, allows to slip by
71 weighty/grave/urgent execution

Ghost	Do not forget. This visitation	110

Is but to whet thy almost blunted purpose.[72]
But, look, amazement[73] on thy mother sits.
O, step between her and her fighting soul!
Conceit[74] in weakest bodies strongest works.
Speak to her, Hamlet.

Hamlet	How is it with you, lady?	115

Gertrude Alas, how is't with you,
That you do bend your eye on vacancy[75]
And with th' incorporal air do hold discourse?[76]
Forth at[77] your eyes your spirits wildly peep,[78]
And as the sleeping soldiers in th' alarm,[79]   120
Your bedded hair like life in excrements
Start up, and stand an end.[80] O gentle son,
Upon the heat and flame of thy distemper[81]
Sprinkle cool patience.[82] Whereon do you look?

Hamlet On him, on him! Look you, how pale he glares!   125
His form and cause conjoined,[83] preaching to stones,
Would make them capable.[84] *(to Ghost)* Do not look upon me,

72 sharpen, urge on your almost dulled purpose
73 bewilderment, distraction
74 thoughts, ideas
75 you direct / turn your eye on nothingness
76 and speak / talk with the immaterial / disembodied air
77 through, from
78 out of control / violently show themselves
79 at the call to arms
80 your hair, spread flat, rises and stands on end like living forms that spring up
   in outgrowths / outshoots
81 disordered / deranged condition
82 composure
83 his figure and motives combined
84 able to understand / respond

Lest with this piteous[85] action you convert

My stern effects.[86] Then what I have to do

130 Will want true color[87] – tears perchance for[88] blood.

Gertrude To whom do you speak this?

Hamlet   Do you see nothing

there?

Gertrude Nothing at all. Yet all that is[89] I see.

Hamlet Nor did you nothing hear?

Gertrude   No, nothing but ourselves.

Hamlet Why, look you there! Look how it[90] steals away!

135 My father, in his habit as he lived!

Look, where he goes, even now, out at the portal![91]

EXIT GHOST

Gertrude This is the very coinage of your brain,

This bodiless creation ecstasy

Is very cunning[92] in.

Hamlet   Ecstasy?

140 My pulse as yours doth temperately[93] keep time,

And makes as healthful music. It is not madness

That I have uttered. Bring me to the test,

---

85 compassionate, tender (possibly "full of piety"?)

86 you turn back/away my severe/rigorous intended deeds

87 will be deprived of/lose/fall short of genuine reason/excuse/justification

88 instead of

89 is there

90 his continued use of "it," rather than "he," underlines Hamlet's profound
   ambiguity toward the Ghost

91 doorway

92 in which madness is very sly/crafty/clever

93 moderately, mildly

And I the matter will re-word,[94] which madness
Would gambol[95] from. Mother, for love of grace,
Lay not that flattering unction[96] to your soul,   145
That not your trespass,[97] but my madness speaks.
It will but skin and film the ulcerous[98] place,
Whiles rank corruption, mining[99] all within,
Infects unseen. Confess yourself to heaven,
Repent what's past, avoid what is to come;   150
And do not spread the compost[100] on the weeds,
To make them ranker. Forgive me this my virtue,
For in the fatness of these pursy[101] times
Virtue itself of vice must pardon beg –
Yea, curb and woo for leave to do him good.[102]   155

Gertrude   O Hamlet, thou hast cleft my heart in twain.

Hamlet   O, throw away the worser part of it
And live the purer with the other half.
Good night—but go not to mine uncle's bed.
Assume[103] a virtue, if you have it not   160
That monster, custom, who all sense doth eat,
Of habits devil,[104] is angel yet in this,

---

94 say again, repeat
95 leap, bound, spring away
96 self-gratifying soothing ointment (the action of anointing with oil, in certain rites of the church)
97 sin, fault ("Forgive us our trespasses, as we forgive those who trespass against us")
98 it will only cover and film over the infected open sore (inner or outer)
99 digging under / away, undermining
100 mold, manure
101 purse-proud, wealthy
102 bow / cringe and woo for permission to do good for vice
103 adopt, simulate, pretend to
104 the devil (Satan) of habits

That to the use[105] of actions fair and good

He likewise gives a frock or livery,[106]

165 That aptly[107] is put on. Refrain to-night,

And that shall lend a kind of easiness

To the next abstinence, the next more easy,

For use almost can change the stamp[108] of nature,

And either [.........][109] the devil, or throw him out

170 With wondrous potency.[110] Once more, good night,

And when you are desirous to be blest,

I'll blessing beg of you. For this same lord,

(*pointing to Polonius*) I do repent, but heaven hath pleased[111]
it so,

To punish me with this[112] and this with me,

175 That I must be their scourge and minister.[113]

I will bestow him, and will answer well[114]

The death I gave him. So again, good night.

I must be cruel, only to be kind.

Thus bad begins and worse remains behind.[115]

One word more, good lady.

180 *Gertrude*   What shall I do?

---

105 performance, practice
106 gives a frock coat/long cloak/cassock/gown/dress or servant's garb
107 appropriately, suitably
108 imprinting (in current usage, "genetic character")
109 a word is missing, probably "welcome," "bring in," or something of the sort
110 power, strength, authority
111 chosen, wanted
112 Polonius's corpse
113 be the heavens' lash/whip and he who administers justice/law/
     punishment
114 dispose of/lodge him and take appropriate responsibility for
115 has yet to come, will follow after

Hamlet Not this, by no means, that I bid[116] you do:
  Let the bloat[117] king tempt you again to bed,
  Pinch wanton[118] on your cheek, call you his mouse,[119]
  And let him, for a pair of reechy kisses,
  Or paddling[120] in your neck with his damned fingers,   185
  Make you to ravel[121] all this matter out,
  That I essentially[122] am not in madness,
  But mad in craft.[123] 'Twere good you let him know,
  For who, that's but a queen — fair, sober, wise —
  Would from a paddock,[124] from a bat, a gib,[125]   190
  Such dear concernings hide?[126] Who would do so?
  No, in despite of sense[127] and secrecy,
  Unpeg[128] the basket on the house's top,
  Let the birds fly[129] and, like the famous[130] ape,
  To try conclusions,[131] in the basket creep,   195

116 forbid
117 flabby, swollen (as a result of self-indulgence)
118 pinch lewdly/lasciviously
119 then, and later, a common term of endearment
120 squalid kisses, or toying, idly/fondly/playfully fingering
121 unwind, reel out (that is, give Hamlet away on "this matter")
122 at bottom, intrinsically
123 but only mad in cunning/guile/ingenuity
124 toad
125 a castrated cat
126 hide such worthy/precious/glorious matters of importance
127 in contempt/disdain of sanity/intelligence/wisdom
128 unfasten, open
129 fly off/away
130 perhaps "famous" then, but unknown now: clearly, however, the
    experimentally minded ape crawls into the bird basket and falls off the
    housetop to his death
131 test the results, conduct an experiment

And break your own neck down.[132]

Gertrude Be thou assured, if words be made of breath,
And breath of life, I have no life to breathe[133]
What thou hast said to me.

Hamlet I must to England. You know that?

200 Gertrude   Alack,[134]
I had forgot. 'Tis so concluded on.[135]

Hamlet There's letters sealed, and my two schoolfellows,
Whom I will trust as I will adders fanged,
They bear the mandate.[136] They must sweep my way
205 And marshal me to knavery.[137] Let it work,
For 'tis the sport to have the engineer
Hoist with his own petard[138] – and 't shall go hard
But I will delve one yard below their mines
And blow them at[139] the moon. O, 'tis most sweet
210 When in one line two crafts directly meet.[140]
This man shall set me packing.[141]

---

132 on the way down
133 speak (that is, "repeat")
134 alas
135 decided
136 will trust as I will adders with fangs, carry the king's commission/orders
137 they must clear my way/provide me with an escort and usher/guide/
conduct me to trickery/roguery; Hamlet is clear that these things are to be
practiced *on* him, not *by* him
138 let it come to pass/be done, because it's fun and games to make the
designer/maker of military devices (bombs) be lifted/blown into the air by
his own bomb
139 it will turn out badly if I don't dig a yard below their barrels of gunpowder,
used like bombs, emplanted below a wall or fort and blow them nearly to
140 in a single/straight line two boats (*and/or* two ingenious/cunning/sly
arts/skills) come face to face (each traveling directly at the other)
141 this corpse will start me carrying/storing a load (*and* plotting, scheming)

I'll lug the guts into the neighbor room.
Mother, good night. Indeed, this counsellor
Is now most still, most secret and most grave,[142]
Who was in life a foolish, prating knave.[143]
Come, sir, to draw toward an end[144] with you.
Good night, mother.

215

    EXEUNT SEVERALLY, FIRST Gertrude, THEN Hamlet,
        DRAGGING Polonius

---

142 heavy, of great weight (*and* highly serious, requiring serious thought, as well
    as headed to his "grave")
143 chattering, /blabbing servant, menial
144 move (and pull) (and lead to) the completion of an action/purpose (*and*
    your death)

Act 4

SCENE I

The castle, that same night

ENTER CLAUDIUS, GERTRUDE, ROSENCRANTZ,
AND GUILDENSTERN

Claudius There's matter in these sighs. These profound heaves[1]
  You must translate: 'tis fit we understand them.
  Where is your son?
Gertrude (*to Rosencrantz and Guildenstern*) Bestow[2] this place on
  us a little while.

EXEUNT ROSENCRANTZ AND GUILDENSTERN

5   Ah, my good lord, what have I seen to-night!
Claudius What, Gertrude? How does Hamlet?
Gertrude Mad as the sea and wind, when both contend
  Which is the mightier. In his lawless fit,
  Behind the arras hearing something stir,

---

1 "profound heaves" = "deep, swelling sigh / wordless utterings"
2 leave us

Whips out his rapier, cries, "A rat, a rat!"   10
And in this brainish apprehension[3] kills
The unseen good old man.

Claudius   O heavy deed!
It had been so with us, had we[4] been there.
His liberty is full of threats to all,
To you yourself, to us, to everyone.   15
Alas, how shall this bloody deed be answered?
It will be laid to us, whose providence
Should have kept short, restrained and out of haunt[5]
This mad young man. But so much was our love
We would not[6] understand what was most fit,   20
But like the owner of a foul disease,
To keep it from divulging, let it feed
Even on the pith[7] of life. Where is he gone?

Gertrude To draw apart[8] the body he hath killed,
O'er whom his very madness, like some ore[9]   25
Among a mineral of metals base,[10]
Shows itself pure. 'A weeps for what is done.

Claudius O Gertrude, come away![11]
The sun no sooner shall the mountains touch
But we will ship him hence, and this vile deed   30

---

3 headstrong and entirely imagined notion
4 the same thing would have happened to me, had I
5 whose prudence/foresight should have restricted/limited and kept away
  from usual/customary places/company
6 did not wish/desire/want to
7 vital part, essence, substance
8 move/drag away/aside
9 mineral containing useful/precious metal (*and* "the metal itself")
10 of inferior quality, worthless
11 leave off (*or* "let us leave this public place")

We must, with all our majesty and skill,
Both countenance and excuse.[12] Ho, Guildenstern!

ENTER ROSENCRANTZ AND GUILDENSTERN

Friends both, go join you with[13] some further aid.
Hamlet in madness hath Polonius slain,
And from his mother's closet hath he dragged him.
Go seek him out. Speak fair,[14] and bring the body
Into the chapel.[15] I pray you, haste in this.

EXEUNT ROSENCRANTZ AND GUILDENSTERN

Come, Gertrude, we'll call up our wisest friends,[16]
And let them know both what we mean to do
And what's untimely done. So haply slander,
Whose whisper o'er the world's diameter,
As level[17] as the cannon to his blank,[18]
Transports his poisoned shot, may miss our name
And hit the woundless[19] air. O, come away!
My soul is full of discord and dismay.

EXEUNT

12 support and apologize for
13 unite, combine in
14 gently, peacefully
15 a private place of worship, common in aristocratic houses
16 summon our wisest supporters
17 horizontally direct
18 the center of its target (a white – "blank" – space at a target's center)
19 incapable of being wounded, invulnerable

SCENE 2

The castle

ENTER HAMLET

Hamlet   Safely stowed.

Rosencrantz, Guildenstern (*from within*) Hamlet! Lord Hamlet!

Hamlet   But soft, what noise? who calls on Hamlet?
O, here they come.

ENTER ROSENCRANTZ AND GUILDENSTERN

Rosencrantz What have you done, my lord, with the dead body?   5

Hamlet   Compounded[1] it with dust, whereto 'tis kin.

Rosencrantz Tell us where 'tis, that we may take it thence[2]
And bear it to the chapel.

Hamlet   Do not believe it.

Rosencrantz Believe what?   10

Hamlet   That I can keep your counsel and not mine own.
Besides, to be demanded of a sponge![3] What replication[4]
should be made by the son of a king?

Rosencrantz Take you me for a sponge, my lord?

Hamlet   Ay, sir, that soaks up the King's countenance,[5] his   15
rewards, his authorities. But such officers do the King best
service, in the end. He keeps them, like an ape,[6] in the corner
of his jaw, first mouthed, to be last swallowed. When he needs

1 put it together with
2 from there / that place
3 peremptorily / imperiously requested by a mercenary hanger-on
4 reply, answer
5 goodwill, favor
6 as an ape does

what you have gleaned, it is but squeezing you and, sponge,
20 you shall be dry again.

Rosencrantz I understand you not, my lord.

Hamlet   I am glad of it: a knavish speech sleeps[7] in a foolish
ear.

Rosencrantz My lord, you must tell us where the body is, and go
25 with us to the King.

Hamlet   The body is with the King, but the King is not
with the body.[8] The King is a thing[9] –

Guildenstern A thing, my lord!

Hamlet   Of nothing. Bring me to him. Hide fox, and all
30 after.[10]

HAMLET RUNS OFF. EXEUNT ALL

7 rests dormant/inert/inactive
8 Hamlet plays with a theory of kingship: the physical king (his "body") and
the power of the kingship are separate. Since the King's powers extend to the
entire castle (and indeed to the entire country), the corpse is necessarily
"with the King." But the corpse is not with the King's body, that is, the King
himself
9 a something, a material object, a piece of property (at which deeply
disrespectful comment – almost heresy – Guildenstern is shocked)
10 the cry, in a child's game such as hide-and-seek

SCENE 3

The castle

ENTER CLAUDIUS, WITH TWO OR THREE ATTENDANT LORDS

Claudius I have sent to seek him, and to find the body.
How dangerous is it that this man goes loose!
Yet must not we put the strong[1] law on him:
He's loved of the distracted[2] multitude,
Who like[3] not in their judgment, but their eyes,   5
And where tis so, th' offender's scourge is weighed,[4]
But never the offence. To bear[5] all smooth and even,
This sudden sending him away must seem
Deliberate pause. Diseases desperate grown
By desperate appliance[6] are relieved,   10
Or not at all.

ENTER ROSENCRANTZ, AND OTHERS

How now? What hath befallen?
Rosencrantz Where the dead body is bestowed, my lord,
We cannot get from him.
Claudius   But where is he?
Rosencrantz Without,[7] my lord, guarded, to know[8] your
pleasure.

1 place upon / apply / impose the emphatic / urgent / severe
2 confused
3 approve, are pleased
4 punishment is considered / measured
5 keep, sustain
6 measures, application, treatment
7 just outside
8 await / learn

Claudius Bring him before us.

15 *Rosencrantz*   Ho! Bring in the lord.

ENTER HAMLET AND GUILDENSTERN

Claudius Now, Hamlet, where's Polonius?

Hamlet At supper.

Claudius At supper? Where?

Hamlet Not where he eats, but where 'a is eaten. A certain
20 convocation of politic worms are e'en[9] at him. Your[10] worm
is your only emperor for diet. We fat all creatures else[11] to fat
us, and we fat ourselves for maggots. Your fat king and your
lean beggar is but variable service[12] – two dishes, but to one
table.

25 That's the end.

Claudius Alas, alas!

Hamlet A man may fish with the worm that hath eat[13] of a
king, and eat[14] of the fish that hath fed of that worm.

Claudius What dost thou mean by this?

30 *Hamlet* Nothing but to show you how a king may go a
progress[15] through the guts of a beggar.

Claudius Where is Polonius?

Hamlet In heaven. Send thither to see. If your messenger find
him not there, seek him i' th' other place yourself. But if

---

9 assembly/synod/meeting of shrewd/prudent/diplomatic worms are even now
10 the
11 fatten all other creatures
12 only a matter of variation in courses being served
13 eaten (then and now "eat" is pronounced, in British English, "et")
14 pronounced in England as it is in the United States
15 a state journey, an official tour

indeed you find him not within this month, you shall nose[16]   35
him as you go up the stairs into the lobby.[17]

Claudius (*to attendants*) Go seek him there.

Hamlet 'A will stay till ye come.

EXEUNT ATTENDANTS

Claudius Hamlet, this deed, for thine especial safety —
Which we do tender as[18] we dearly grieve   40
For that which thou hast done — must send thee hence
With fiery quickness. Therefore prepare thyself.[19]
The bark is ready, and the wind at help,
Th' associates tend, and everything is bent[20]
For England.

Hamlet   For England?

Claudius   Ay, Hamlet.

Hamlet   Good.   45

Claudius So is it, if thou knew'st our purposes.[21]

Hamlet I see a cherub[22] that sees them. But, come, for
England! Farewell, dear mother

Claudius Thy loving father, Hamlet.

Hamlet My mother. Father and mother is man and wife.   50
Man and wife is one flesh — and so: my mother. Come, for
England!

EXIT

Dark humor, Quibbles/Puns

16 (1) smell, (2) confront, face, (3) rub / press the nose against, examine
17 passage, corridor, covered walk
18 offer just as
19 make yourself ready / pack what you will need
20 favorable / useful, your comrades wait, and everything is set / bound
21 intentions, plans
22 one of the second order of angels, especially endowed with knowledge

madness: loss of inner order

Claudius Follow him at foot;[23] tempt him with speed aboard.

Delay it not. I'll have him hence tonight.

55 Away! For everything is sealed and done

That else leans on th'affair. Pray you, make haste.

EXEUNT ROSENCRANTZ AND GUILDENSTERN

And, England, if my love thou hold'st at aught[24] –

As my great power thereof may give thee sense,[25]

Since yet thy cicatrice looks raw and red

60 After[26] the Danish sword, and thy free awe

Pays homage to us[27] – thou mayst not coldly set

Our sovereign process,[28] which imports at full,

By letters congruing to[29] that effect,

The present death of Hamlet. Do it, England,

65 For like the hectic[30] in my blood he rages,

And thou must cure me. Till I know 'tis done,

Howe'er my haps,[31] my joys were ne'er[32] begun.

EXIT

23 close to him
24 favor/approval you consider of any worth whatever
25 as my (Denmark's) great strength/armies might make you aware
26 your scar (from a healed wound) still looks raw and red subsequent to/
    following after England's encounter with
27 willing/voluntary terror/dread pays deference to us (acknowledgment of
    superiority *and* money paid)
28 consider with indifference our authoritative/kingly command
29 conveys/communicates/states full/in detail by letters in harmony with
30 fever
31 fortune, fate
32 will never be

SCENE 4
A plain in Denmark

ENTER FORTINBRAS AND SOLDIERS

Fortinbras Go, captain, from me greet the Danish king.
  Tell him that, by his licence, Fortinbras
  Craves the conveyance[1] of a promised[2] march
  Over his kingdom. You know the rendezvous.
  If that his Majesty would aught with us,   5
  We shall express our duty in his eye.[3]
  And let him know so.
Captain   I will do't, my lord.
Fortinbras Go softly on.[4]

EXEUNT FORTINBRAS AND SOLDIERS

ENTER HAMLET, ROSENCRANTZ, GUILDENSTERN,
AND OTHERS

Hamlet Good sir, whose powers[5] are these?
Captain They are of Norway, sir.   10
Hamlet How purposed, sir, I pray you?
Captain Against some part[6] of Poland.
Hamlet Who commands them, sir?
Captain The nephew to old Norway, Fortinbras.

1 passage, with an escort
2 previously declared
3 I will set forth my due respect / homage in his sight / presence
4 proceed at a comfortable / easy pace
5 armies, forces
6 section, region

15 *Hamlet*   Goes it against the main[7] of Poland, sir,
     Or for some frontier?
    Captain   Truly to speak, and with no addition,[8]
     We go to gain a little patch of ground
     That hath in it no profit but the name.[9]
20   To pay five ducats, five,[10] I would not farm it,
     Nor will it yield to Norway or the Pole
     A ranker rate,[11] should it be sold in fee.[12]
    Hamlet   Why, then the Polack never will defend it.
    Captain   Yes, it is already garrisoned.
25 *Hamlet*   Two thousand souls and twenty thousand ducats
     Will not debate[13] the question of this straw.[14]
     This is th' imposthume[15] of much wealth and peace,
     That inward breaks, and shows no cause without
     Why the man dies. I humbly thank you, sir.
    Captain   God bye you, sir.

EXIT

30 *Rosencrantz*   Wilt please you go, my lord?
    Hamlet   I'll be with you straight. Go a little before.[16]

EXEUNT ALL BUT HAMLET

7 chief part
8 something added for reasons of style
9 (that is, making it part of Norway rather than part of Poland)
10 in rent
11 larger sum/amount
12 outright
13 abate, end, settle
14 trifle, insignificance
15 boil, pimple, ulcer
16 ahead

How all occasions do inform[17] against me
And spur my dull revenge! What is a man,
If his chief good and market[18] of his time
Be but to sleep and feed? A beast, no more.   35
Sure he that made us with such large discourse,[19]
Looking before and after, gave us not
That capability and god-like reason
To fust[20] in us unused. Now, whether it be
Bestial oblivion, or some craven scruple[21]   40
Of thinking too precisely on th' event[22] –
A thought which, quartered, hath but one part wisdom
And ever[23] three parts coward – I do not know
Why yet I live to say "This thing's to do,"
Sith I have cause, and will, and strength, and means   45
To do't. Examples gross as earth exhort[24] me.
Witness this army of such mass and charge[25]
Led by a delicate and tender[26] prince,
Whose spirit with divine ambition puffed[27]
Makes mouths at[28] the invisible event,[29]   50

17 circumstances/events lodge complaints
18 value
19 reasoning, understanding
20 turn moldy/stale
21 cowardly/frightened doubt/uncertainty
22 outcome, result
23 always
24 large/plain/obvious as earth incite/admonish/urge
25 great size and cost/price/expense
26 skillful/ingenious and youthful
27 driven, impelled
28 makes faces at/shows contempt for
29 the unseeable outcome

Exposing what is mortal and unsure
To all that fortune, death and danger dare —
Even for an egg-shell. Rightly[30] to be great
Is not to stir without great argument,[31]
55   But greatly to find quarrel in a straw
When honor's at the stake. How stand I then,
That have a father killed, a mother stained —
Excitements of my reason and my blood[32] —
And let all sleep, while to my shame I see
60   The imminent death of twenty thousand men
That, for a fantasy and trick[33] of fame,
Go to their graves like[34] beds, fight for a plot
Whereon the numbers cannot try the cause,[35]
Which[36] is not tomb enough and continent[37]
65   To hide the slain? O, from this time forth,
My[38] thoughts be bloody, or be nothing worth!

EXIT

---

30 correctly
31 reason, thought
32 incentives/excitements to action for my reason and my passions/emotions
    (*and* family/race/kin)
33 phantom/illusion and sham appearance/deceptive show
34 as if to their
35 on which the many men fighting cannot (in so small a space) test the reason
    for the action
36 which patch of ground
37 a big-enough tomb and container
38 let my

SCENE 5
The castle

ENTER GERTRUDE, HORATIO, AND A GENTLEMAN[1]

Gertrude   I will not speak with her.

Gentleman She is importunate, indeed distract.[2]
Her mood will needs be pitied.[3]

Gertrude   What would she have?

Gentleman She speaks much of her father, says she hears
There's tricks[4] i' the world, and hems, and beats her heart,   5
Spurns enviously at straws,[5] speaks things in doubt[6]
That carry but half sense. Her speech is nothing,
Yet the unshaped[7] use of it doth move
The hearers to collection.[8] They aim at it,
And botch[9] the words up fit[10] to their own thoughts,   10
Which — as her winks, and nods, and gestures yield[11] them —
Indeed would make one think there might be thought,
Though nothing sure, yet much unhappily.[12]

1 a man of gentle birth serving as a court official
2 troubled in mind, confused
3 state of mind must be pitied
4 frauds, deceptions, shams, hoaxes
5 unpleasantly/with great ill-will kicks at/rejects trifles/things of no
  significance
6 uncertainly/hesitantly/fearfully
7 formless, shapeless
8 inferences
9 guess/try (some texts have "yawn," meaning "gape")
10 patch/clumsily mend the words according to
11 produce, deliver
12 unfortunately, regrettably

Horatio 'Twere good she were[13] spoken with, for she may strew[14]

15   Dangerous conjectures in ill-breeding[15] minds.

Gertrude Let her come in.

EXIT HORATIO

(*aside*) To my sick soul, as sin's true nature is,

Each toy[16] seems prologue to some great amiss.[17]

So full of artless jealousy[18] is guilt,

20   It spills[19] itself in fearing to be spilt.

ENTER OPHELIA

Ophelia Where is the beauteous Majesty of Denmark?

Gertrude How now, Ophelia!

Ophelia (*sings*)

How should I your true love know
    From another one?
25   By his cockle hat[20] and staff,
    And his sandal shoon.[21]

Gertrude Alas, sweet lady, what imports[22] this song?

13 if she were
14 spread, sprinkle
15 unmannerly, given to mischief
16 trifle, minor / insignificant thing
17 fault, evil deed
18 clumsy / ignorant / simple-minded suspicion / mistrust / fear
19 destroys, ruins, kills
20 traditional headwear of religious pilgrim and lovers
21 sandals too were pilgrim and lover associated
22 means

Ophelia Say you? Nay, pray you, mark.

(SINGS)

He is dead and gone, lady,
  He is dead and gone.   30
At his head a grass-green turf,
  At his heels a stone.²³

O ho!
Gertrude Nay, but, Ophelia –
Ophelia Pray you, mark.   35

(SINGS)

White his shroud as the mountain snow –

ENTER CLAUDIUS

Gertrude Alas, look here, my lord.
Ophelia (*sings*)

Larded²⁴ with sweet flowers
Which bewept to the grave did [not²⁵] go
  With true-love²⁶ showers.²⁷   40

Claudius How do you, pretty lady?
Ophelia Well, God 'ild²⁸ you! They say the owl was a baker's

---

23 burial stone, grave marker
24 covered, heaped high, decorated
25 a much-debated word, deleted in some texts
26 *either* Herb Paris, a kind of lily, *or* ornaments/symbols of true love
27 in showers (that, many/a lot of flowers) (the song, like the singer, is
    confused)
28 yield: reward

daughter.[29] Lord, we know what we are, but know not what
we may be. God be at your table!

45 *Claudius* Conceit[30] upon her father.

Ophelia Pray, let's have no words[31] of[32] this, but when they ask
you what it means, say you this:

(SINGS)

To-morrow is Saint Valentine's day,
All in the morning betime,[33]
50 And I a maid at[34] your window,
To be your Valentine.

Then up he rose, and donned his clothes,
And dupped the chamber door,[35]
Let in the maid, that out a maid[36]
55 Never departed more.[37]

Claudius Pretty Ophelia.

Ophelia Indeed, la, without an oath, I'll make an end on't:

(SINGS)

By Gis[38] and by Saint Charity,

---

29 a legend: a baker's daughter who refused to give Christ bread was
transformed into an owl
30 morbid seizure of the mind
31 no speech/talk? or no argument?
32 about
33 early
34 standing? knocking?
35 opened the bedroom door
36 a virgin
37 again
38 shortened form of "Jesus"

Alack, and fie for shame!
Young men will do't, if they come to't.   60
   By Cock,[39] they are to blame.

Quoth she, "before you tumbled me,[40]
   You promised me to wed."

He answers:

"So would I ha' done, by yonder sun,   65
   An[41] thou hadst not come to my bed."

Claudius   How long hath she been thus?
Ophelia   I hope all will be well. We must be patient, but I
cannot choose but weep, to think they should lay him i' the
cold ground. My brother shall know of it. And so I thank you   70
for your good counsel. Come, my coach! Good night, ladies,
good night. Sweet ladies, good night, good night.

[handwritten: → post the point of no return
Purpose!
madness = cause]

EXIT

King Claudius Follow her close. Give her good watch,[42]
   I pray you.

EXIT GENTLEMAN

O, this is the poison of deep grief: it springs   75
All from her father's death. – And now behold!
O Gertrude, Gertrude,
When sorrows come, they come not single spies

---

39 (1) God, and (2) penis
40 threw me on the ground: had sexual intercourse with me
41 if
42 guard, vigilance

*military
violence*

But in battalions. First, her father slain.

80 Next, your son gone, and he most violent author[43]

Of his own just remove.[44] The people muddied,

Thick[45] and unwholesome in their thoughts and whispers,

For good Polonius' death — and we have done but greenly

In hugger-mugger[46] to inter him. Poor Ophelia

85 Divided from herself and her fair judgment,[47]

Without the which we are pictures, or mere beasts.[48]

Last, and as much containing[49] as all these,

Her brother is[50] in secret come from France,

Feeds on his wonder, keeps himself in clouds,[51]

90 And wants not buzzers to infect[52] his ear

With pestilent speeches of[53] his father's death,

Wherein necessity, of matter beggared,

Will nothing stick our person to arraign

In ear and ear.[54] O my dear Gertrude, this,

95 Like to a murd'ring-piece, in many places

55

---

43 instigator, begetter

44 upright/fair/well-deserved departure/exile

45 muddled/confused, thick-headed/stupid

46 and, also, because of what we have done very unskillfully in secret/
disorderly fashion

47 obvious good sense/discernment

48 empty/soulless representations of human beings, or no more than animals/
brute creatures

49 containing as much

50 has

51 feeds on his perplexity/astonishment, keeps himself suspicious/lost in his
imaginings

52 does not lack rumormongers to influence/corrupt

53 with poisonous/noxious/deadly speeches about

54 deprived of any substance/facts, will in no way stop/delay/hesitate to
accuse me in one ear after another

Gives me superfluous death.[55]

A NOISE WITHIN; ENTER A GENTLEMAN

Gertrude   Alack, what noise is this?

Claudius   Where are my Switzers?[56] Let them guard the door.

(*to Gentleman*) What is the matter?

Gentleman   Save yourself, my lord.

The ocean, overpeering of his list,[57]

Eats not the flats with more impetuous[58] haste   100

Than young Laertes, in a riotous head,

O'erbears[59] your officers. The rabble call him lord,

And, as[60] the world were now but to[61] begin,

Antiquity forgot, custom not known,

The ratifiers and props of every word,[62]   105

They cry, "Choose we! Laertes shall be king!"

Caps, hands, and tongues applaud it to the clouds:

"Laertes shall be king, Laertes king!"

Gertrude   How cheerfully on the false trail they cry![63]

O, this is counter,[64] you false[65] Danish dogs![66]   110

---

55 like a cannon firing scattering shot (like shrapnel), here and there and
   everywhere, pointlessly kills me
56 Swiss mercenaries, often used by European royalty as palace guards
57 looking down on / towering over / dominating his borders, shores
58 does not gnaw away at the level ground with more violent haste
59 with a noisy / unrestrained / turbulent insurgent mob, overcomes / overthrows
60 as if
61 just be about to
62 they the ones who confirm / approve and uphold / every command / order
63 like hunting dogs following a scent
64 hunting dogs running away from, rather than toward, the hunted animal
   (that is, following the scent backward, along the path the prey has already
   taken)
65 treacherous / defective / mistaken
66 worthless cowards

(NOISE WITHIN)

Claudius The doors are broke.

ENTER LAERTES AND OTHERS

Laertes Where is this king? (*to others*) Sirs, stand you all
without.[67]

Others No, let's come in!

Laertes   I pray you, give me leave.[68]

Others We will, we will.

Laertes I thank you. Keep[69] the door.

EXEUNT OTHERS

115 *Laertes*   O thou vile king,
Give me my father!

Gertrude   Calmly, good Laertes.

Laertes That drop of blood that's calm proclaims me bastard,[70]
Cries cuckold[71] to my father, brands the harlot
Even here, between the chaste unsmirchèd brow
Of my true mother.[72]

120 *Claudius*   What is the cause, Laertes,
That[73] thy rebellion looks so giant-like?[74]

---

67 all of you remain outside
68 your consent
69 watch / guard / defend
70 illegitimate, not my father's true son
71 that is, that Polonius was the husband of an unfaithful wife
72 brands (literally) the word "harlot," right here in the middle of the unsoiled,
  unstained forehead of my faithful, honest mother
73 why, Laertes, does
74 huge (like the rebellion of the ancient giants against the then-king of the
  gods)

(*to Gertrude*) Let him go, Gertrude. Do not fear[75] our person.
There's such divinity doth hedge[76] a king
That treason can but peep to[77] what it would,
Acts little of his will.[78] Tell me, Laertes,   125
Why thou art thus incensed. (*to Gertrude*) Let him go,
    Gertrude.
(*to Laertes*) Speak, man.

Laertes   Where is my father?
Claudius   Dead.
Gertrude   But not by him.
Claudius (*to Gertrude*) Let him demand his fill.
Laertes   How came he dead? I'll not be juggled[79] with.   130
To hell allegiance![80] Vows,[81] to the blackest devil!
Conscience and grace, to the profoundest pit![82]
I dare[83] damnation. To this point I stand,
That both the worlds I give to negligence,[84]
Let come what comes — only I'll be revenged   135
Most thoroughly for my father.
Claudius   Who shall stay you?
Laertes   My will,[85] not all the world.

---

75 be afraid for
76 defend, surround, protect
77 look through a narrow aperture, or half-closed eyes, at what it wishes
78 and does little of what it wants
79 deceived by tricks, cheated, beguiled
80 I vow allegiance to hell
81 I make my vows
82 God's grace / favor / mercy I consign to the deepest pit
83 challenge, defy
84 I remain steadfast / firm, that earth and heaven I consign to indifference /
    neglect
85 by my will

And for my means, I'll husband[86] them so well
They shall go far with little.

Claudius   Good Laertes,
140   If you desire to know the certainty[87]
Of your dear father's death, is't writ in your revenge
That, swoopstake,[88] you will draw[89] both friend and foe,
Winner and loser?

Laertes   None but his enemies.

Claudius   Will you know[90] them, then?
145   **Laertes**   To his good friends thus wide I'll ope my arms
And like the kind life-rend'ring pelican
Repast[91] them with my blood.

Claudius   Why, now you speak
Like a good child and a true gentleman.
That I am guiltless of your father's death,
150   And am most sensibly[92] in grief for it,
It shall as level[93] to your judgment 'pear[94]
As day does to your eye.

Others   (*within*) Let her come in.

Laertes   How now? What noise is that?

ENTER OPHELIA

86 as for my resources / money, I'll prudently manage
87 the facts, the truth
88 indiscriminately, helter-skelter (sweeping up all the stakes at once)
89 drag out, hunt down
90 do you want to know
91 naturally self-sacrificing pelican (thought to feed its young on its own
   blood) I'll feed
92 intensely, acutely
93 intelligible
94 appear

O heat, dry up my brains! Tears seven times salt[95]
Burn out the sense and virtue[96] of mine eye!   155
By heaven, thy madness shall be paid with weight,
Till our scale turn the beam.[97] O rose of May,
Dear maid, kind sister, sweet Ophelia!
O heavens, is't possible a young maid's wits
Should be as mortal as an old man's life?[98]   160
Nature is fine[99] in love, and where 'tis fine
It sends some precious instance[100] of itself
After the thing it loves.

Ophelia (*sings*)

They bore him barefaced[101] on the bier.[102]
   Hey non nonny, nonny, hey nonny.   165
And in his grave rained many a tear –

Fare you well, my dove!

Laertes Hadst thou thy wits, and didst persuade revenge,
   It could not move[103] thus.
Ophelia You must sing "A-down a-down, an you call him a-   170
   down-a." O, how the wheel becomes[104] it! It is the false

95 seven times as salty as salt
96 feeling and strength/power
97 in full, until the balance bar of our scale swings downward
98 the old man in question is Polonius
99 exquisitely fashioned, delicately structured
100 sign, token
101 face uncovered
102 movable stand for holding a corpse and for carrying it to the grave
103 urge/strongly advise revenge, it could not be as emotionally affecting as
    this
104 refrain fits, goes well with

steward that stole his master's daughter.

Laertes   This nothing's more than matter.[105]

Ophelia (*to Laertes*) There's rosemary, that's for remembrance.
175   Pray you, love, remember. And there is pansies. That's for
    thoughts.

Laertes   A document[106] in madness, thoughts and
    remembrance fitted.

Ophelia (*to Gertrude*) There's fennel for you, and columbines.[107]
180   (*to Claudius*) There's rue for you, and here's some for me.[108]
    We may call it herb of grace o' Sundays.[109] O you must wear
    your rue with a difference.[110] There's a daisy.[111] I would give
    you some violets,[112] but they withered all when my father
    died. They say 'a made a good end.

(SINGS)

185   For bonny sweet Robin is all my joy.

Laertes   Thought and affliction, passion, hell itself,
    She turns to favor[113] and to prettiness.

Ophelia (*sings*)

    And will 'a not come again?

---

105 devoid of sense, this means more than words with meaning
106 lesson, warning
107 herbs sometimes associated with unfaithfulness in marriage
108 herb sometimes associated with repentance, sorrow
109 herb of virtue on Sundays
110 (?) heraldically, "difference" refers to a marker indicating a junior/lesser
    branch of a family, thus clearly separating that branch from the chief line,
    and that has been suggested as the meaning here
111 a flower sometimes associated with dissembling
112 sometimes associated with faithfulness
113 charm

And will 'a not come again?
    No, no, he is dead,   190
    Go to thy death-bed.
He never will come again.

His beard was as white as snow,
All flaxen was his poll.[114]
    He is gone, he is gone,   195
    And we cast away[115] moan.
God ha' mercy on his soul!

And of all Christian souls, I pray[116] God. God bye[117] ye.

EXIT

Laertes   Do you see this, O God?
Claudius Laertes, I must commune with your grief,   200
Or you deny me right.[118] Go but apart,
Make choice of[119] whom your wisest friends you will,
And they shall hear and judge 'twixt you and me.
If by direct or by collateral[120] hand
They find us touched,[121] we will our kingdom give,   205
Our crown, our life, and all that we call ours,
To you in satisfaction.[122] But if not,

114 the top of his head
115 throw away, discard
116 for all Christian souls, I pray to
117 redeem
118 share/participate in (*or* confer/talk intimately about) your grief, or else
      you deny me justice
119 just go yourself, choose among
120 indirect, subordinate
121 me stained, connected
122 payment of a debt

Be you content to lend your patience to us,
And we shall jointly labor with your soul
To give it due content.

210 *Laertes*   Let this be so.
His means of death, his obscure funeral —
No trophy,[123] sword, nor hatchment[124] o'er his bones,
No noble[125] rite nor formal ostentation[126] —
Cry to be heard, as 'twere from heaven to earth,
That I must call't in question.[127]

215 *Claudius*   So you shall.
And where th' offense[128] is, let the great axe[129] fall.
I pray you, go with me.

EXEUNT

123 hidden/humble funeral — no monument/memorial
124 no tablet bearing the deceased's coat of arms (fastened on the front of his
     home and, after the funeral, on his tomb)
125 illustrious, splendid
126 display, show, ceremony
127 require an examination of it
128 crime, sin
129 the executioner's axe and/or God's axe

SCENE 6

The castle

ENTER HORATIO AND A GENTLEMAN

Horatio   What[1] are they that would speak with me?

Gentleman Seafaring men, sir. They say they have letters for you.

Horatio   Let them come in.

EXIT GENTLEMAN

    I do not know from what part of the world

    I should be greeted,[2] if not from Lord Hamlet.   5

ENTER SAILORS

First Sailor God bless you, sir.

Horatio   Let Him bless thee too.

First Sailor 'A shall, sir, an't[3] please Him. There's a letter for you,

    sir. It came from th'ambassador that was bound for England —

    if your name be Horatio, as I am let[4] to know it is.   10

Horatio   (*reads*) "Horatio, when thou shalt have overlooked[5]

    this, give these fellows some means[6] to the king. They have

    letters for him. Ere we were two days old at sea, a pirate of

    very warlike appointment[7] gave us chase. Finding ourselves

    too slow of sail, we put on a compelled valor, and in the   15

---

1 of what nature, condition, class
2 addressed
3 if it
4 permitted, allowed
5 perused, read
6 opportunity for communicating with
7 outfitting

grapple[8] I boarded them. On the instant they got clear[9] of
our ship, so I alone became their prisoner. They have dealt
with me like thieves of mercy,[10] but they knew what they
did: I am to do a good turn for them. Let the King have the
20   letters I have sent, and repair[11] thou to me with as much
speed as thou wouldst fly[12] death. I have words to speak in
thine ear will make thee dumb,[13] yet are they much too light
for the bore[14] of the matter. These good fellows will bring
thee where I am. Rosencrantz and Guildenstern hold their
25   course for England: of them I have much to tell thee.
Farewell.

    "He that thou knowest thine, HAMLET."

Come, I will give you way[15] for these your letters,
And do't the speedier, that[16] you may direct me
30   To him from whom you brought them.

EXEUNT

8 assumed a necessary/obligatory boldness/bravery/courage, and in the
   close-in combat
9 at that moment they got free
10 a turning-on-its-head of the proverbial phrase "angels of mercy"
11 make your way, come
12 flee from
13 strike you dumb/confound/nonplus you
14 too small/not heavy enough for the caliber/size
15 a means of delivery
16 and I will do it the speedier, so that

SCENE 7
The castle

ENTER CLAUDIUS AND LAERTES

Claudius Now must your conscience my acquittance seal,[1]
And you must put me in your heart for friend,
Sith you have heard, and with a knowing[2] ear,
That he which hath your noble father slain
Pursued my life.

Laertes   It well appears. But tell me   5
Why you proceeded not against these feats,
So crimeful and so capital[3] in nature,
As by your safety, wisdom, all things else,[4]
You mainly were stirred up.

Claudius   O, for two special reasons;
Which may to you, perhaps, seem much unsinewed,[5]   10
But yet to me they are strong. The queen his mother
Lives almost by his looks, and for myself —
My virtue or my plague,[6] be it either which[7] —
She is so conjunctive[8] to my life and soul
That, as the star moves not but in his sphere,   15

---

1 my release from debt (moral debt: therefore a declaration of his innocence)
   affirm/finalize
2 informed/knowledgeable/aware
3 surprising tricks/facts, so steeped in evil/sin and so deadly/deserving of
   death
4 all other things, you were
5 feeble, weak
6 my merit/moral excellence or my affliction/calamity
7 whichever of the two
8 connected, united

I could not but by her.[9] The other motive
Why to a public count[10] I might not go
Is the great love the general gender[11] bear him,
Who, dipping[12] all his faults in their affection,
20   Would, like the spring that turneth wood to stone,[13]
Convert his gyves to graces,[14] so that my arrows,
Too slightly timbered for so loud[15] a wind,
Would have reverted[16] to my bow again,
And not where I had aimed them.

25   *Laertes*   And so have I a noble father lost,
A sister driven into desp'rate terms,[17]
Whose worth, if praises may go back[18] again,
Stood challenger on mount[19] of all the age
For her perfection. But my revenge will come.

30   *Claudius*   Break not your sleeps for that. You must not think
That we are[20] made of stuff so flat and dull[21]
That we can let our beard be shook with danger.[22]
And I think it pastime. You shortly shall hear more.
I loved your father, and we love ourself,
35   And that, I hope, will teach you to imagine –

9 could not move except according to/in harmony with her
10 accounting, reckoning
11 the multitude, the common sort/people
12 immersing, dyeing
13 such springs were known in England, the water containing so much lime
    they could petrify wood
14 his shackles/fetters/chains to charms
15 made of wood too slender/insubstantial for so strong/clamorous
16 returned, come back
17 hopeless/awful condition/circumstances
18 back in time
19 on a high hill/military breastwork
20 I am
21 so insipid/slow-witted/stupid and listless/muffled/obtuse
22 pulled back and forth by mischief

ENTER A MESSENGER

How now? What news?

Messenger   Letters, my lord, from Hamlet.
These to your Majesty, this to the Queen.

Claudius   From Hamlet? Who brought them?

Messenger Sailors, my lord, they say. I saw them not:
They were given me by Claudio.[23] He received them   40
Of him that brought them.

Claudius   Laertes, you shall hear them.
(*to Messenger*) Leave us.

EXIT MESSENGER

(*reads*) "High and mighty, you shall know I am set naked[24] on
your kingdom. To-morrow shall I beg leave to see your kingly
eyes, when I shall, first asking your pardon thereunto, recount   45
the occasion of my sudden and more strange return. Hamlet."

What should this mean? Are all the rest come back?
Or is it some abuse, and no such thing?[25]

Laertes   Know you the hand?[26]

Claudius   'Tis Hamlet's character.[27]
"Naked!"
And in a postscript here, he says "alone."   50
Can you devise[28] me?

Laertes   I'm lost in it, my lord. But let him come.

___

23 a court official, otherwise unnamed
24 destitute, unarmed, unprotected
25 deceit/imposture, and no such thing has in fact happened
26 handwriting
27 writing
28 explain/figure out/resolve it for

It warms the very sickness in my heart
That I shall live and tell him to his teeth,
"Thus did'st thou."

55 *Claudius*   If it be so, Laertes —
As how should it be so? How otherwise? —
Will you be ruled by me?

Laertes   Ay, my lord,
So you will not o'errule me to a peace.

Claudius To thine own peace. If he be now returned,
60 As checking at his voyage,[29] and that he means
No more to undertake it, I will work him
To an exploit,[30] now ripe in my device,
Under the which he shall not choose but fall,[31]
And for his death no wind of blame shall breathe,
65 But even his mother shall uncharge the practice[32]
And call it accident.

Laertes   My lord, I will be ruled —
The rather if you could devise it so
That I might be the organ.[33]

Claudius   It falls right.[34]
You have been talked of since your travel much,
70 And that in Hamlet's hearing, for a quality[35]
Wherein, they say, you shine. Your sum of parts[36]

29 it being the case that he has turned back from
30 bring/manipulate him to an act, deed
31 my plan, in the operation of which he cannot help but die
32 acquit the deed/scheme/treachery of any guilt (uncharge: not charge)
33 instrument/actively operating tool
34 it works out naturally/correctly/exactly
35 skill, ability
36 the totality of your talents/personal qualities/abilities

Did not together pluck such envy from him
As did that one, and that, in my regard,
Of the unworthiest siege.[37]

Laertes   What part is that, my lord?

Claudius A very riband[38] in the cap of youth,   75
Yet needful too, for youth no less becomes
The light and careless livery[39] that it wears
Than settled age his sables and his weeds,[40]
Importing health and graveness.[41] Two months since,
Here was a gentleman of Normandy –   80
I've seen myself, and served against, the French,
And they can[42] well on horseback—but this gallant[43]
Had witchcraft in't. He grew unto his seat,
And to such wondrous doing brought his horse
As he had been incorpsed and demi-natured   85
With the brave[44] beast. So far he topped[45] my thought
That I, in forgery[46] of shapes and tricks,[47]
Come short of what he did.

Laertes   A Norman was't?

37 distinction, rank, status
38 a genuine ribbon
39 harmonizes with/befits the graceful/frivolous and negligent/artless style of
   dress
40 dark (usually black) clothing, as also worn for mourning
41 signifying spiritual/moral/mental soundness and importance/authority
42 know how/have the capacity to do
43 polished, courtierlike gentleman
44 made into one body with, and half-endowed with the nature of the splendid
   animal
45 exceeded
46 mentally inventing/fabricating (notions of what could be done on
   horseback)
47 forms, arrangements and feats of dexterity/skill

    Claudius A Norman.

    Laertes   Upon my life, Lamord.

90 *Claudius*   The very same.

    Laertes   I know him well. He is the brooch[48] indeed

      And gem of all the nation.

    Claudius He made confession of you,[49]

      And gave you such a masterly report[50]

95   For art and exercise in your defence,

      And for your rapier most especially,

      That he cried out 'twould be a sight indeed

      If one[51] could match you. The scrimers[52] of their nation,

      He swore, had had neither motion, guard, nor eye,[53]

100   If you opposed them. Sir, this report of his

      Did Hamlet so envenom with his envy

      That he could nothing do but wish and beg

      Your sudden coming o'er, to play[54] with him.

      Now, out of this –

    Laertes   What out of this, my lord?

105 *Claudius* Laertes, was your father dear to you?

      Or are you like the painting[55] of a sorrow,

      A face without a heart?

    Laertes   Why ask you this?

    Claudius Not that I think you did not love your father,

48 ornament
49 acknowledged that he knew you
50 an account of your masterly capabilities
51 anyone
52 fencers
53 movements/moves, defensive stances, nor perception/ range of vision
54 perform, sport, practice
55 two-dimensional image

But that I know love is begun by time,
And that I see, in passages of proof,   110
Time qualifies[56] the spark and fire of it.
There lives within the very flame of love
A kind of wick or snuff[57] that will abate it,
And nothing is at a like goodness still,[58]
For goodness, growing to a plurisy,   115
Dies in his own too-much.[59] That we would do
We should do when we would, for this "would" changes
And hath abatements[60] and delays as many
As there are tongues, are hands, are accidents,[61]
And then this "should" is like a spendthrift sigh[62]   120
That hurts by easing. But to the quick o' the ulcer.[63]
Hamlet comes back: what would you undertake
To show yourself your father's son in deed
More than in words?

Laertes   To cut his throat i' the church.

Claudius No place, indeed, should murder sanctuarize.[64]   125
Revenge should have no bounds. But, good Laertes,
Will you do this? Keep close[65] within your chamber:

56 proven instances, time modifies/diminishes
57 charred part of the wick, no longer able to burn and thus negatively affecting the burning of the uncharred portion
58 that will lower/diminish/destroy it, and nothing is always of the same goodness
59 goodness, growing to a fullness/excess, dies in its own overabundance
60 decreases, diminishings
61 as there are interfering tongues, as there are hands, as there are accidents
62 foolish/wasteful sigh (sighing could thin the blood and kill, even though it "eased" sorrow/pain)
63 actively/vigorously alive part of the purulent open sore
64 shelter, protect (violence was forbidden on sacred ground)
65 stay shut up/secret

Hamlet returned shall know you are come home.
We'll put on[66] those shall praise your excellence
130 And set a double varnish on the fame[67]
The Frenchman gave you, bring you in fine together
And wager on your heads.[68] He, being remiss,
Most generous and free from all contriving,[69]
Will not peruse the foils,[70] so that, with ease,
135 Or with a little shuffling,[71] you may choose
A sword unbated, and in a pass of practice
Requite[72] him for your father.

Laertes   I will do't:
And, for that purpose, I'll anoint[73] my sword.
I bought an unction of a mountebank,[74]
140 So mortal that, but dip a knife in it,
Where it draws blood no cataplasm so rare,[75]
Collected from all simples that have virtue
Under the moon, can save the thing[76] from death
That is but scratched withal.[77] I'll touch my point
145 With this contagion, that if I gall him slightly,

66 urge/egg on
67 put a double shine/glow on the reputation
68 finally bring you together and bet on who will win
69 careless/inattentive, highly gallant and free of all plotting, scheming
70 swords used in fencing
71 shifting about, manipulation
72 not having its point covered, and in the thrusts of a practice bout repay
73 rub something on it
74 ointment/unguent from an itinerant quack (pretender to medical skill)
75 poultice/plaster ("medicine") so exceptional
76 herbs used for medicinal purposes, having power enhanced by the moon's magic, can save anything
77 therewith

It may[78] be death.

Claudius Let's further think of[79] this,
    Weigh what convenience both of time and means
    May fit us to our shape.[80] If this should fail,
    And that our drift look through our bad performance,[81]   150
    'Twere better not essayed.[82] Therefore this project
    Should have a back or second, that might hold
    If this should blast in proof.[83] Soft! let me see.
    We'll make a solemn wager on your cunnings.[84]
    I ha't![85]   155
    When in your motion[86] you are hot and dry –
    As make your bouts more violent[87] to that end –
    And that he calls for drink, I'll have prepared him
    A chalice for the nonce,[88] whereon but sipping,
    If he by chance escape your venomed stuck,[89]   160
    Our purpose may hold there.—But stay, what noise?

ENTER GERTRUDE

---

78 contagious poison, so that if I barely scratch him, it will have the power to kill
79 about
80 agreed-upon arrangements both of time and operation may be appropriate to our plan
81 our purpose/aim/object be visible/show through our defective actions
82 tried, attempted
83 backup or second plan, that might work if this should fail when put to the test
84 the abilities/skills of you and Hamlet
85 have it
86 bodily exertion
87 therefore make your fencing involve more physical exertion
88 drinking cup/goblet for the occasion
89 thrust

Gertrude One woe doth tread upon another's heel,

So fast they follow. Your sister's drowned, Laertes.

Laertes   Drowned! O, where?

165 *Gertrude* There is a willow grows askant the brook,

That shows his hoar[90] leaves in the glassy stream.

Therewith fantastic garlands did she make

Of crow-flowers,[91] nettles, daisies, and long purples[92]

That liberal[93] shepherds give a grosser name,

170 But our cold maids[94] do dead men's fingers call them.

There on the pendent boughs her crownet weeds[95]

Clambering to hang, an envious sliver[96] broke,

When down her weedy trophies[97] and herself

Fell in the weeping[98] brook. Her clothes spread wide,

175 And mermaid-like awhile they bore her up,

Which time she chanted snatches of old lauds,[99]

As one incapable of her own distress,[100]

Or like a creature native and indued

Unto that element.[101] But long it could not be

180 Till that her garments, heavy with their drink,

Pulled the poor wretch from her melodious lay[102]

90 that grows aslant the brook, which displays / exhibits its gray-white
91 buttercups
92 wild orchids with purple spikes (also known as dead men's fingers)
93 free-speaking, lewd
94 less heated virgins
95 hanging boughs her garlands woven with flowers
96 grudging / malicious twig / small branch
97 skillfully made decorative objects
98 tear-full (that is, both wet and sorrowing)
99 sang bits and pieces / portions of old hymns / songs of praise
100 not aware / insensible of her own anguish / affliction
101 brought up in water
102 song

To muddy death.

Laertes   Alas, then, she is drowned?

Gertrude Drowned, drowned.

Laertes   Too much of water hast thou, poor Ophelia,
    And therefore I forbid[103] my tears. (*weeps*) But yet   185
    It is our trick;[104] nature her custom[105] holds,
    Let shame say what it will. When these are gone,
    The woman[106] will be out. Adieu, my lord.
    I have a speech o' fire, that fain would blaze,
    But that this folly douts it.[107]

EXIT LAERTES

Claudius   Let's follow, Gertrude.   190
    How much I had to do to calm his rage!
    Now fear I this will give it start again.
    Therefore let's follow.

EXEUNT

103 hold back, restrain
104 human beings' way
105 habit
106 these tears are gone, the woman in me
107 of weeping extinguishes it

Act 5

A churchyard

ENTER TWO CLOWNS, THE FIRST ONE BEING
THE GRAVEDIGGER

Clown 1 Is she to be buried in Christian burial, when she
   wilfully seeks her own salvation?

Clown 2 I tell thee she is, and therefore make her grave straight.
   The crowner hath sat on her, and finds it[1] Christian burial.

5   *Clown 1* How can that be, unless she drowned herself in her
   own defense?

Clown 2 Why, 'tis found so.

Clown 1 It must be "se offendendo."[2] It cannot be else. For here
   lies the point: if I drown myself wittingly, it argues an act,[3]

10   and an act hath three branches – it is,[4] to act; to do, to

---

1 at once. The coroner has conducted his hearing on her, and determines,
   declares it
2 self-defense: an unlearned error for "se defendendo"
3 knowingly, consciously, it declares / determines
4 components, divisions—which are

perform. Argal,[5] she drowned herself wittingly.

Clown 2 Nay, but hear you,[6] Goodman[7] Delver[8] –

Clown 1 Give me leave.[9] Here lies the water – good. Here
stands the man – good. If the man go to this water, and
drown himself, it is, will he, nill he,[10] he goes. Mark you that.   15
But if the water come to him and drown him, he drowns not
himself. Argal, he that is not guilty of his own death shortens
not his own life.

Clown 2 But is this law?

Clown 1 Ay, marry, is't – crowner's quest[11] law.   20

Clown 2 Will you ha' the truth on't? If this had not been a
gentlewoman,[12] she should have been buried out o' Christian
burial.

Clown 1 Why, there thou say'st.[13] And the more pity that great
folk should have countenance[14] in this world to drown or   25
hang themselves, more than their even-Christen.[15] Come, my
spade. There is no ancient gentlemen but gard'ners, ditchers,[16]
and grave makers. They hold up[17] Adam's profession.[18]

---

5 thus: an unlearned error for "ergo"
6 listen
7 a form of address: a yeoman
8 an occupational label: a digger
9 with your permission, allow me
10 if he wishes or he does not wish to: willy-nilly
11 inquest, inquiry
12 a lady, of good birth / breeding
13 that's exactly right
14 position, standing
15 fellow Christians
16 those who dig / repair ditches
17 preserve, abide by
18 "Whan Adam dalf [dug], / And Eve span [spun], / Who was thanne / A
gentilman?" Cited in Thomas Walsingham (1322–88), *Historia Anglicana:* this
little poem has a very long history

Clown 2 Was he a gentleman?

30 *Clown 1* 'A was the first that ever bore arms.[19]

Clown 2 Why, he had none.

Clown 1 What, art a heathen? How dost thou understand[20] the
Scripture? The Scripture says Adam digged. Could he dig
without arms? I'll put another question to thee. If thou
35 answerest me not to the purpose,[21] confess thyself[22] –

Clown 2 Go to.[23]

Clown 1 What is he that builds stronger than either the mason,
the shipwright, or the carpenter?

Clown 2 The gallows-maker, for that frame[24] outlives a
40 thousand tenants.

Clown 1 I like thy wit[25] well, in good faith. The gallows does
well.[26] But how does it well?[27] It does well to those that do
ill. Now thou dost ill to say the gallows is built stronger than
the church. Argal, the gallows may do well to thee. To't[28]
45 again, come.

Clown 2 Who builds stronger than a mason, a shipwright, or a
carpenter?

Clown 1 Ay, tell me that, and unyoke.[29]

---

19 possessed a heraldic coat of arms
20 interpret the language of
21 in terms of the point at issue / the matter in hand
22 confess thyself (admit the charge), and be hanged: a proverb
23 come, come
24 structure
25 cleverness, quickness
26 as an answer to riddling question he had asked
27 how does it work well / do good (all Elizabethans loved wordplay)
28 try it
29 (you can) stop working

Clown 2 Marry, now I can tell.

Clown 1 To't.   50

Clown 2 Mass,[30] I cannot tell.

ENTER HAMLET AND HORATIO, AT A DISTANCE

Clown 1 Cudgel[31] thy brains no more about it, for your dull ass
will not mend his pace with[32] beating. And when you are
asked this question next, say "a grave-maker: the houses he
makes last till doomsday." Go, get thee to Yaughan:[33] fetch me   55
a stoup[34] of liquor.

EXIT CLOWN 2

CLOWN 1 DIGS AND SINGS

In youth, when I did love, did love,
    Methought it was very sweet
To contract[35] – O – the time for – a – my behove,[36]
    O, methought, there – a – was nothing – a – meet.[37]   60

Hamlet Has this fellow no feeling of[38] his business? 'A sings in
grave-making.

Horatio Custom hath made it in him a property of easiness.[39]

30 by the Mass
31 beat (cudgel: club)
32 because a stupid donkey will not improve/better his pace because of
33 the name of an innkeeper (?)
34 tankard (a tall mug with a handle and, often, a lid); *also* pail, bucket
35 agree, enter into
36 my use/benefit
37 suitable
38 emotions about
39 habit has made it, in him, something comfortable

Hamlet 'Tis e'en so. The hand of little employment hath the
65 daintier sense.⁴⁰

Clown 1 (*sings*)

> But age, with his stealing⁴¹ steps,
>   Hath clawed me in his clutch,⁴²
> And hath shipped me into the land,⁴³
>   As if I had never been such.⁴⁴

HE THROWS UP A SKULL

70 *Hamlet* That skull had a tongue in it, and could sing once.
How the knave jowls⁴⁵ it to the ground, as if 'twere Cain's
jaw-bone, that⁴⁶ did the first murder! This might be the pate
of a politician, which this ass now o'er- offices,⁴⁷ one⁴⁸ that
would circumvent⁴⁹ God, might it not?

75 *Horatio* It might, my lord.

Hamlet Or of a courtier; which could say "Good morrow,
sweet lord! How dost thou, sweet lord?" This might be Lord
Such-a-One, that⁵⁰ praised my Lord Such-a-One's horse,

40 leisure (that is, the hand that does not work much) has more fastidious
    feelings
41 thieving (*or* secret) steps, has
42 grip, grasp
43 packed me off into the countryside / rural regions (?)
44 what I once was
45 knocks, strikes
46 which did (Cain was supposed to have killed Abel with the jawbone of a
    donkey)
47 skull / head of a crafty schemer / intriguer, which this ignorant fellow now
    lords it over
48 the living man from whom the skull originated
49 get the better of ("o'er-reach")
50 the courtier? one (lesser?) lord speaking of another lord?

when 'a meant to beg[51] it, might it not?

Horatio   Ay, my lord.   80

Hamlet   Why, e'en so. And now my Lady Worm's, chapless, and
knocked about the mazzard[52] with a sexton's spade. Here's
fine revolution, an we had the trick[53] to see't. Did these
bones cost no more the breeding, but to play at loggats[54] with
'em? Mine[55] ache to think on't.   85

Clown 1   (*sings*)

A pick-axe, and a spade, a spade,
   For and[56] a shrouding sheet.
O, a pit of clay for to be made
   For such a guest is meet.

HE THROWS UP ANOTHER SKULL

Hamlet   There's another. Why may not that be the skull of a   90
lawyer? Where be his quiddities[57] now, his quillevies, his cases,
his tenures, and his tricks?[58] Why does he[59] suffer [60] this rude
knave now to knock him about the sconce[61] with a dirty

51 beg for
52 her skull, having no lower jaw, and knocked about the head / face
53 cyclical change / overturning, if we had the art / skill
54 in the production, or just to play a game in which small pieces of wood were
   thrown, to see who could get them closest to a designated target-object
55 my bones
56 and also, plus
57 quibbling, picky arguments ("quidditas?" = "what is the essence / nature of
   ———?")
58 his citations to old cases, his land-lease contracts, and his strategems, clever
   contrivances
59 the hypothetical lawyer
60 allow, permit
61 head

shovel, and will not tell him of his action of battery?[62] Hum!

95 This fellow[63] might be in's time a great buyer of land, with
his statutes,[64] his recognizances,[65] his fines,[66] his double
vouchers,[67] his recoveries.[68] Is this the fine of his fines, and
the recovery[69] of his recoveries, to have his fine pate full of
fine[70] dirt? Will his vouchers vouch[71] him no more of his

100 purchases, and double ones too, than the length and breadth
of a pair of indentures?[72] The very conveyances[73] of his lands
will hardly lie in this box,[74] and must th' inheritor[75] himself
have no more, ha?

Horatio Not a jot[76] more, my lord.

105 *Hamlet* Is not parchment made of sheepskins?

Horatio Ay, my lord, and of calf-skins too.

Hamlet They are sheep and calves which[77] seek out assurance[78]

---

62 a lawsuit brought for assault
63 the next skull to be tossed up
64 governmental enactments/laws
65 his acknowledgments/ bonds
66 a fictitious, collusive suit, used instead of a straightforward conveyance of
   land
67 trickily substituting, in a legal proceeding, one person for another
68 a legal maneuver to get around entailed restrictions on the sale of land
69 end of his fines, and the restoring/regaining
70 delicately ground-up ("loose, powdery")
71 affirm, attest, guarantee
72 agreements, contracts, deeds
73 documents for transfers/purchases and sales of land, kept in a deed box
74 fit in this deed box/coffin
75 the "heir" (in the fictive transactions already referred to?)
76 a very small part of anything
77 who
78 (1) legal proof of a transfer of land, (2) the actual, uninterrupted ownership
   of land: it is foolish, considering the obvious evidence of human mortality, to
   expect that the first-named can guarantee the second

in that. I will speak to this fellow. (*to Clown 1*) Whose grave's
this, sirrah?[79]

Clown 1 Mine, sir.   110

(SINGS)

O, a pit of clay for to be made
    For such a guest is meet.

Hamlet I think it be thine, indeed, for thou liest in't.

Clown 1 You lie out on't, sir, and therefore it is not yours. For
my part, I do not lie in't, and yet it is mine.   115

Hamlet 'Thou dost lie in't, to be in't and say it is thine. 'Tis for
the dead, not for the quick.[80] Therefore thou liest.

Clown 1 'Tis a quick lie, sir. 'Twill away again, from me to you.

Hamlet What man dost thou dig it for?

Clown 1 For no man, sir.   120

Hamlet What woman, then?

Clown 1 For none, neither.

Hamlet Who is to be buried in't?

Clown 1 One that was a woman, sir. But rest her soul, she's dead.

Hamlet (*to Horatio*) How absolute the knave is! We must speak   125
by the card, or equivocation[81] will undo us. By the Lord,
Horatio, this three years I have took note of it. The age is
grown so pickèd[82] that the toe of the peasant comes so near
the heel of the courtier, he galls his kibe.[83] – (*to Clown 1*)

79 form of address used for speaking down to someone
80 living (and quick-witted)
81 the mariner's chart (*or* his compass), or ambiguity
82 picky, finicky, fastidious
83 the peasant hurts/injures the sore on the back of the courtier's heel

130   How long hast thou been a grave-maker?

Clown 1 Of all the days i' the year, I came to't that day that our
last king Hamlet overcame Fortinbras.[84]

Hamlet   How long is that since?

Clown 1 Cannot you tell that? Every fool can tell that. It was the
135   very day that young Hamlet was born, he that is mad, and
sent into England.

Hamlet   Ay, marry, why was he sent into England?

Clown 1 Why, because 'a was mad. 'A shall recover his wits
there, or, if 'a do not, it's no great matter there.

140 *Hamlet*   Why?

Clown 1 'Twill not be seen in him there. There the men are as
mad as he.

Hamlet   How came he mad?

Clown 1 Very strangely, they say.

145 *Hamlet*   How strangely?

Clown 1 Faith, e'en[85] with losing his wits.

Hamlet   Upon what ground?[86]

Clown 1 Why, here in Denmark. I have been sexton here, man
and boy, thirty years.

150 *Hamlet*   How long will a man lie i' the earth ere he rot?

Clown 1 Faith, if he be not rotten before he die – as we have
many pocky corses now-a-days, that will scarce hold the
laying in[87] – 'a will last you some eight year or nine year. A
tanner[88] will last you nine year.

---

84 the older Fortinbras
85 precisely
86 for what reason (*or* "earth, land")
87 since we have many syphilitic corpses these days, which will barely endure
being laid in the grave
88 one who tans/cures hides/leather

Hamlet   Why he more than another?   155

Clown 1 Why, sir, his hide is so tanned with his trade, that he
will keep out water a great while, and your water is a sore[89]
decayer of your whoreson[90] dead body. Here's a skull now
hath lien you[91] i' th' earth three and twenty years.

Hamlet   Whose was it?   160

Clown 1 A whoreson mad fellow's it was. Whose do you think it
was?

Hamlet   Nay, I know not.

Clown 1 A pestilence[92] on him for a mad rogue! 'A poured a
flagon of Rhenish on my head once. This same skull, sir, was   165
Yorick's skull, the king's jester.

Hamlet   This?

Clown 1 E'en that.

Hamlet   Let me see. (*takes the skull*) Alas, poor Yorick! I knew
him, Horatio — a fellow of infinite jest, of most excellent   170
fancy.[93] He hath borne me on his back a thousand times. And
now how abhorred[94] in my imagination it is! My gorge rises
at it.[95] Here hung those lips that I have kissed I know not
how oft. (*to the skull*) Where be your gibes now? Your
gambols?[96] Your songs? Your flashes of merriment, that were   175
wont to set the table on a roar?[97] Not one now, to mock your

89 grievous
90 a common imprecation, in current usage something like "bastard" or "s.o.b."
91 been lying
92 plague
93 imagination, whimsy
94 disgusting, horrid: abHORRED (?)
95 the vomit rises in my throat, at the thought
96 where be your taunts/scoffing now? your leaping about/dancing?
97 habitually/usually set everyone at the table laughing loudly/boisterously

own grinning?[98] Quite chap-fallen?[99] Now get you to my
lady's chamber, and tell her, let her paint an inch thick, to this
favor[100] she must come. Make her laugh at that. Prithee,
180   Horatio, tell me one thing.
  Horatio   What's that, my lord?
  Hamlet   Dost thou think Alexander[101] looked o' this fashion i'
  th' earth?
  Horatio   E'en so.
185   *Hamlet*   And smelt so? Pah!

PUTS DOWN THE SKULL

  Horatio   E'en so, my lord.
  Hamlet   To what base[102] uses we may return, Horatio! Why may
  not imagination trace the noble dust of Alexander, till he find
  it stopping a bung-hole?[103]
190   *Horatio*   'Twere to consider too curiously,[104] to consider so.
  Hamlet   No, faith, not a jot; but to follow him thither with
  modesty enough, and likelihood to lead[105] it. As thus:
  Alexander died, Alexander was buried, Alexander returneth
  into dust, the dust is earth, of earth we make loam,[106] and

98 the "grinning" skull is proverbial
99 lower jaw hanging down, in despair and having no lower jaw ("chap" or
   "chop": lower jaw)
100 appearance, look, aspect, countenance (face)
101 Alexander the Great, 356–323 B.C.
102 lowly, degraded
103 hole at the top of a cask, "corked" by a "bung"
104 contemplate / think about too elaborately / minutely
105 moderation / self-control, and probability / promise of success to conduct /
   direct / guide
106 compound of clay or other dirt, plus water, sand, and so on

why of that loam, whereto he was converted, might they not   195
stop a beer-barrel?[107]

Imperious[108] Caesar, dead and turned to clay,
Might stop a hole to keep the wind away:
O, that that earth[109] which kept the world in awe,
Should patch a wall to expel the winter's flaw![110]   200
But soft! but soft awhile. Here comes the King,
The Queen, the courtiers.

    ENTER BEARERS, WITH COFFIN, A PRIEST, LAERTES,
      CLAUDIUS, GERTRUDE, THEIR ATTENDANTS, &C

                    Who is this they follow?
And with such maimèd rites?[111] This doth betoken[112]
The corse they follow did with desp'rate hand
Fordo its own life.[113] 'Twas of some estate.   205
Couch[114] we awhile, and mark.

        RETIRES WITH HORATIO

Laertes What ceremony else?
Hamlet   That is Laertes,
A very noble youth. Mark.

---

107 into which he was turned/transformed, might they not close/seal a beer-
     barrel
108 imperious (*and* imperial)
109 Alexander (men were made by God from/out of dust/dirt/earth)
110 keep out the winter's blast, gust
111 as mourners and with such crippled/cut-off/incomplete rites
112 point to, signal, be a sign of
113 did with despairing/hopeless/reckless hand end/do away with its own life
114 degree of rank/dignity/status. Let us hide, conceal

Laertes What ceremony else?

210 Priest   Her obsequies[115] have been as far enlarged
      As we have warranty. Her death was doubtful,[116]
      And but that great command o'ersways[117] the order,
      She should in ground unsanctified have lodged[118]
      Till the last trumpet. For charitable prayers,
215   Shards,[119] flints and pebbles should be thrown on her,
      Yet here she is allowed her virgin crants,
      Her maiden strewments,[120] and the bringing home
      Of bell and burial.[121]

Laertes Must there no more be done?

Priest   No more be done.
220   We should profane[122] the service of the dead
      To sing sage requiem and such rest[123] to her
      As to peace-parted[124] souls.

Laertes   Lay her i' the earth.
      And from her fair and unpolluted flesh
      May violets spring! I tell thee, churlish[125] priest,

115 funeral rites
116 authorization/official sanction. Her manner of death was questionable/
      ambiguous
117 eminent/high/elevated/lofty power/coercion overrules
118 resided
119 in spite of the fact that charitable prayers, fragments of broken earthenware,
120 her wreaths/garlands, her maiden flowers, and so on, scattered on the grave
121 bringing her home to heaven, with the ringing of church bells and church-
      sanctioned burial
122 desecrate, violate
123 solemn requiem and the same kind of repose/tranquillity to her
124 those who peacefully departed/were separated from earthly existence
125 rude, low-bred

A minist'ring angel shall my sister be   225
When thou liest howling.[126]
Hamlet   What, the fair Ophelia!
Gertrude Sweets to the sweet. Farewell!

SCATTERING FLOWERS

I hoped thou shouldst have been my Hamlet's wife.
I thought thy bride-bed to have decked,[127] sweet maid,
And not have strewed thy grave.
Laertes   O, treble woe   230
Fall ten times treble on that cursèd head
Whose wicked deed[128] thy most ingenious sense[129]
Deprived thee of! Hold off the earth awhile,
Till I have caught her once more in mine arms.[130]

LEAPS INTO THE GRAVE

Now pile your dust upon the quick and dead   235
Till of this flat[131] a mountain you have made
To o'ertop[132] old Pelion[133] or the skyish head
Of blue Olympus.
Hamlet (advancing) What is he whose grief
Bears such an emphasis? whose phrase of sorrow   240

126 in hell
127 imagined/fancied I would adorn/beautify your bride-bed
128 killing Polonius
129 the intelligent/able/talented mind
130 coffins were often left open
131 level ground
132 rise above/higher than
133 giants piled this Greek mountain on Mount Ossa, then piled Ossa-Pelion
    on top of Mount Olympus, while trying to reach and overthrow the gods

Conjures the wand'ring stars[134] and makes them stand
Like wonder-wounded hearers? This is I,
Hamlet the Dane.

HE LEAPS INTO THE GRAVE[135]

Laertes　　　　　　　　The devil take thy soul!

HE GRAPPLES[136] WITH HAMLET

Hamlet　Thou pray'st not well.
245　I prithee, take thy fingers from my throat,
For though I am not splenitive[137] and rash,
Yet have I something in me dangerous,[138]
Which let thy wiseness fear. Hold off[139] thy hand.
Claudius　Pluck them asunder.
Gertrude　　　　　　　　Hamlet, Hamlet!
All　　　Gentlemen!
250　*Horatio*　(*to Hamlet*) Good my lord, be quiet.[140]

ATTENDANTS PART THEM

Hamlet　Why, I will fight with him upon this theme
Until my eyelids will no longer wag.
Gertrude　O my son, what theme?
Hamlet　I loved Ophelia. Forty thousand brothers
255　Could not, with all their quantity of love,

134　strong/imprecise rhetoric? whose sorrowful language calls upon/invokes
　　the wandering planets
135　some texts do not contain this stage direction
136　fights
137　irritable, peevish, ill-humored
138　unsafe, hazardous, injurious
139　take away
140　peaceful, still, silent

Make up my sum. (*to Laertes*) What wilt thou do for her?

Claudius   O, he is mad, Laertes.

Gertrude   For love of God, forbear[141] him.

Hamlet   'Swounds, show me what thou'lt do.

Woo't[142] weep? woo't fight? woo't fast? woo't tear[143] thyself?   260

Woo't drink up eisel?[144] eat a crocodile?

I'll do't. Dost thou come here to whine?

To outface[145] me with leaping in her grave?

Be buried quick with her, and so will I.

And if thou prate[146] of mountains, let them throw   265

Millions of acres on us, till our ground,[147]

Singeing his pate against the burning zone,[148]

Make Ossa like a wart! Nay, an thou'lt mouth,[149]

I'll rant as well as thou.

Gertrude   This is mere[150] madness,

And thus awhile the fit will work on him.   270

Anon, as patient as the female dove

When that her golden couplets are disclosed,[151]

His silence will sit drooping.

Hamlet   (*to Laertes*) Hear you, sir.

141 hold/keep back
142 will you
143 lacerate, wound
144 vinegar
145 to make high-pitched, querulous noises? to outdo/defy
146 talk idly, chatter to no effect
147 the ground/earth piled on top of us
148 the orbit of the sun
149 declaim pompously, oratorically
150 pure, sheer, absolute
151 yellow/golden downy pair of chicks (doves were said to lay two eggs) are
     hatched

What is the reason that you use[152] me thus?

275 I loved you ever.[153] But it is no matter.

Let Hercules himself do what he may,

The cat will mew and dog will have his day.

EXIT

Claudius I pray you, good Horatio, wait upon[154] him.

EXIT HORATIO

(*to Laertes*) Strengthen your patience in[155] our last night's speech.

280 We'll put the matter to the present push.[156]

Good Gertrude, set some watch over your son.

This grave shall have a living[157] monument.

An hour of quiet[158] shortly shall we see;

Till then, in patience our proceeding[159] be.

EXEUNT

152 treat, behave toward
153 always
154 attend to
155 by means / in thoughts of
156 thrust, stroke, vigorous attempt
157 lasting, enduring
158 a time of peace / tranquillity
159 actions, doings

SCENE 2
The castle

ENTER HAMLET AND HORATIO

Hamlet So much for this, sir. Now shall you see[1] the other.
    You do remember all the circumstance?
Horatio Remember it, my lord!
Hamlet Sir, in my heart there was a kind of fighting,
    That would not let me sleep. Methought I lay   5
    Worse than the mutines in the bilboes.[2] Rashly —
    And praised be rashness for it. Let us know
    Our indiscretion[3] sometimes serves us well,
    When our deep plots do pall.[4] And that should teach us
    There's a divinity that shapes our ends,   10
    Rough-hew[5] them how we will —
Horatio   That is most certain.
Hamlet Up from my cabin,
    My sea-gown scarfed[6] about me, in the dark
    Groped I to find out them, had my desire,[7]
    Fingered their packet, and in fine[8] withdrew   15
    To mine own room again, making so bold,

1 learn, consider
2 the mutineers in long shackles (attached, on shipboard, to fixed iron bars)
3 let us keep in mind that our imprudence
4 when our weighty/dangerous plans weaken/fail
5 which should teach us there's a divinity that directs/orders our purposes/
   destinies, rough-cut them
6 loose garment of coarse cloth wrapped around me like a scarf
7 to locate Rosencrantz and Guildenstern, did as I wished (found them
   sleeping)
8 pilfered/stole their package of official documents, and in conclusion/finally

My fears forgetting manners, to unseal
Their grand commission,[9] where I found, Horatio –
O royal knavery! – an exact command,
20   Larded[10] with many several sorts of reasons
Importing[11] Denmark's health, and England's too,
With, ho! such bugs and goblins in my life[12]
That, on the supervise, no leisure bated[13] –
No, not to stay the grinding[14] of the axe –
My head should be struck off.

25 *Horatio*   Is't possible?
Hamlet Here's the commission: read it at more leisure.
But wilt thou hear now how I did proceed?
Horatio I beseech you.
Hamlet Being thus be-netted round with villanies –
30   Ere I could make a prologue[15] to my brains,
They[16] had begun the play – sat me down,
Devised a new commission, wrote it fair.[17]
I once did hold it, as our statists[18] do,
A baseness[19] to write fair and labored much

---

9 high charge/instructions
10 an express/detailed command, garnished/fattened
11 suggesting reasons/matters of
12 bogeys/scarecrows/assorted imaginary terrors and dangers in my continued
    existence
13 upon reading (these instructions), no opportunity for delay allowed
14 to wait for the sharpening
15 an introduction, preface
16 his brains
17 clean, clear (like the writing of copyists and office clerks)
18 statesmen, politicians
19 something low, degraded, shabby

How to forget that learning,[20] but, sir, now   35
It did me yeoman's[21] service. Wilt thou know
The effect of what I wrote?

Horatio   Ay, good my lord.

Hamlet An earnest conjuration[22] from the King,
As England was his faithful tributary,
As love between them like the palm might flourish,[23]   40
As peace should still her wheaten[24] garland wear
And stand a comma[25] 'tween their amities,[26]
And many such-like as's of great charge,[27]
That on the view and knowing of these contents,[28]
Without debatement further more or less,[29]   45
He should those bearers[30] put to sudden death,
Not shriving-time[31] allowed.

Horatio   How was this sealed?

Hamlet Why, even in that was heaven ordinant.[32]

---

20 how to have an "interesting/impressive" handwriting rather than a readily legible one
21 good, efficient, useful
22 serious/weighty charge/call
23 "The righteous shall flourish like the palm tree": Psalm 92.12
24 wheat as a symbol of prosperity/plenty is traditionally associated with representations of Peace
25 variously understood as "pause/interval," *or* "link," *or* "something tiny/insignificant" *or* "separate but still connected"
26 friendly relations
27 many repeated uses of "as," of great weight/importance
28 that immediately after reading and becoming aware of this intention
29 without discussion/argument, completely/exactly as instructed
30 Rosencrantz and Guildenstern
31 confession and absolution
32 directing, ordaining

I had my father's signet in my purse,[33]
50   Which was the model of that Danish seal,[34]
Folded the writ up in form of th' other,[35]
Subscribed[36] it, gave't the impression,[37] placed it safely,[38]
The changeling[39] never known. Now, the next day
Was our sea-fight, and what to this was sequent[40]
55   Thou know'st already.

Horatio So Guildenstern and Rosencrantz go to't.[41]

Hamlet Why, man, they did make love to this employment.
They are not near my conscience; their defeat
Does by their own insinuation grow.[42]
60   'Tis dangerous when the baser nature comes
Between the pass and fell incensèd points[43]
Of mighty opposites.[44]

Horatio   Why, what a king is this!

Hamlet Does it not, think'st thee, stand me now upon[45] –
He that hath killed my king and whored my mother,

---

33 small seal, usually set into a ring, in my money-pouch
34 a copy of the well-known (larger, somewhat more formal) Danish seal
35 the document I had written just like the original commission / instructions
36 signed it, using the King's name
37 sealed it with wax, on which the seal was "impressed / stamped"
38 securely back in Rosencrantz and Guildenstern's "packet"
39 thing substituted for another thing
40 following
41 die
42 not closely affecting my conscience; their undoing / ruin grows from their own stealthy self-introduction
43 when the inferior nature comes between the thrust (as in fencing) and the fierce / terrible / ruthless burning / angry blades, swords
44 here, Hamlet and the King
45 now become incumbent on / necessary for me

Popped[46] in between th' election and my hopes,[47]   65
Thrown out his angle for my proper life,
And with such coz'nage[48] – is't not perfect conscience
To quit[49] him with this arm? And is't not to be damned
To let this canker of our nature come
In further evil?[50]   70

Horatio It must be shortly known to him from England
What is the issue[51] of the business there.

Hamlet It will be short.[52] The interim[53] is mine,
And a man's life's no more than to say[54] "one."
But I am very sorry, good Horatio,   75
That to Laertes I forgot myself,
For by the image of my cause I see
The portraiture[55] of his.[56] I'll court his favors.[57]
But sure the bravery[58] of his grief did put me
Into a tow'ring passion.

Horatio   Peace. Who comes here?   80

ENTER OSRIC, A COURTIER

46 come unexpectedly/suddenly
47 to be elected king himself
48 gone fishing for my own life, and with such perfect cheating/defrauding
49 faultless good conscience to repay him with this arm?
50 and wouldn't I be damned to allow this ulcer of human nature to achieve
    further evil?
51 outcome
52 a brief time
53 period between then and now
54 count
55 image
56 they both want revenge
57 goodwill
58 bravado, show, display

Osric   Your lordship is right welcome back to Denmark.

Hamlet I humbly thank you, sir. (*to Horatio*) Dost know this
water-fly?

Horatio (*aside*) No, my good lord.

85   *Hamlet* (*aside*) Thy state is the more gracious, for 'tis a vice[59] to
know him. He hath much land, and[60] fertile. Let a beast be
lord of beasts, and his crib shall stand at the king's mess.[61] 'Tis
a chough,[62] but as I say, spacious[63] in the possession of dirt.

Osric   Sweet lord, if your lordship were at leisure, I should
90   impart[64] a thing to you from his Majesty.

Hamlet I will receive it, sir, with all diligence of spirit.[65] Put
your bonnet[66] to his[67] right use. 'Tis for the head.[68]

Osric   I thank your lordship. It is very hot.

Hamlet No, believe me, 'tis very cold. The wind is northerly.

95   *Osric*   It is indifferent[69] cold, my lord, indeed.

Hamlet But yet methinks it is very sultry and hot – for my
complexion.[70]

Osric   Exceedingly, my lord. It is very sultry, as 'twere – I

---

59 situation/condition is all the more attractive/happy, for it is an indulgence
  in vice
60 and that
61 stall will stand at the King's table (a good-sized company of diners is
  implied)
62 he is like a small, chattering, crowlike bird
63 ample
64 make known, communicate
65 careful attention
66 men's and boys' caps
67 its
68 not for waving about, as Osric has been doing
69 tolerably
70 nature, temperament

cannot tell how. But, my lord, his Majesty bade me signify to
you that 'a has laid a great wager on your head. Sir, this is the   100
matter —

Hamlet *(indicating that Osric should put on his hat)* I beseech you,
remember.

Osric   Nay, good my lord: for mine ease,[71] in good faith. Sir,
here is newly come to court Laertes — believe me, an absolute   105
gentleman, full of most excellent differences, of very soft
society and great showing.[72] Indeed, to speak feelingly of
him, he is the card or calendar of gentry,[73] for you shall find
in him the continent of what part a gentleman would see.[74]

Hamlet Sir, his definement suffers no perdition[75] in you, though   110
I know to divide him inventorially would dozy th' arithmetic
of memory,[76] and yet but yaw neither, in respect of his quick
sail.[77] But, in the verity of extolment, I take him to be a soul
of great article,[78] and his infusion of such dearth and rareness
as, to make true diction of him, his semblable is his mirror,   115

---

71 Osric would rather not put on his hat; "ease" = "comfort" — but this is the
     highly conventional language of courtly politeness
72 a perfect / complete gentleman, full of most excellent distinctions, of very
     easy / pleasing manners and distinguished outward appearance
73 to speak warmly of him, he is the map / chart or guide / model of good
     breeding / courtesy
74 the container / receptacle of whatever aspect a gentleman might want to see
75 his characterization / description suffers no loss, diminution
76 list / enumerate separately each of his qualities would stupefy / confuse
     memory's computational / arithmetic capabilities
77 cause neither (arithmetic nor memory) to go off course (*or* still cause no
     straying from a straight course), in view of / because of his lively / vigorous
     sailing capacities / abilities
78 to praise (him) truthfully / sincerely / honestly, I consider him a soul of large
     size / capabilities

and who else would trace him, his umbrage,[79] nothing more.

Osric   Your lordship speaks most infallibly[80] of him.

Hamlet The concernancy,[81] sir? Why do we wrap the
gentleman in our more rawer[82] breath?

120 *Osric*   Sir?

Horatio Is't not possible to understand in another tongue?[83] You
will to't,[84] sir, really.

Hamlet What imports the nomination[85] of this gentleman?

Osric   Of Laertes?

125 *Horatio* (*aside*) His purse is empty already. All's golden words are
spent.[86]

Hamlet Of him, sir.

Osric   I know you are not ignorant –

Hamlet I would you did,[87] sir. Yet, in faith, if you did, it would
130   not much approve[88] me. Well, sir?

Osric   You are not ignorant of what excellence Laertes is –

Hamlet I dare not confess that, lest I should compare[89] with him
in excellence. But to know a man well were[90] to know
himself.

---

79 his essence (*or* quality) of such scarcity and uncommonness/unusualness
   that, to speak truly of him, his only likeness is the image of himself, and he
   who/anyone who wishes to draw/copy him is his semblance/shadow
80 unfailingly, with utter certainty
81 business at hand, matter at issue
82 words/breath that is cruder, more uncultivated than is Laertes himself
83 another language (like plain English)
84 you'll get there
85 what signifies/means the naming
86 all his precious/important words are used up
87 wish you did know that I was not ignorant/unlearned
88 recommend/commend (Osric being himself a fool)
89 be compared
90 would be

Osric I mean, sir, for his weapon.[91] But in the imputation[92]   135
laid on him by them, in his meed he's unfellowed.[93]

Hamlet What's his weapon?

Osric Rapier and dagger.

Hamlet That's two of his weapons. But well.[94]

Osric The king, sir, hath wagered with him six Barbary horses,   140
against the which he has impawned, as I take it, six French
rapiers and poniards, with their assigns, as girdle, hangers, and
so.[95] Three of the carriages,[96] in faith, are very dear to fancy,
very responsive[97] to the hilts, most delicate[98] carriages, and of
very liberal conceit.[99]   145

Hamlet What call you the carriages?

Horatio (*aside*) I knew you must be edified by the margent[100] ere
you had done.

Osric The carriages, sir, are the hangers.

Hamlet The phrase would be more german[101] to the matter, if   150
we could carry cannon by our sides.[102] I would it might be

---

91 understood here as a plural: weapons
92 prestige/reputation
93 honor/distinction he has none who is his equal
94 well and good (never mind)
95 six Arab horses, against the which Laertes has risked, as I understand it, six
French rapiers and daggers, with their accessories, as belts, straps/loops
(which let the weapon hang from the weapon-belt), and so on
96 that which carries (a pompous way of saying "hangers")
97 very pleasing to/esteemed by good taste/critical judgment, very well
matched with, harmonious
98 fine, subtle, ingenious
99 of free/inventive conception/design
100 instructed/spiritually improved by the commentary ("marginal
comments")
101 germane, relevant
102 gun carriages: the support and transport structures for cannon

"hangers" till then. But, on.[103] Six Barbary horses against six
French swords, their assigns, and three liberal-conceited
carriages: that's the French bet against the Danish. Why is this
155   "impawned," as you call it?

Osric   The king, sir, hath laid, sir, that in a dozen passes[104]
between yourself and him, he shall not exceed you[105] three
hits. He hath laid on twelve for nine. And it would come to
immediate trial,[106] if your lordship would vouchsafe[107] the
160   answer.

Hamlet How[108] if I answer "no"?

Osric   I mean, my lord, the opposition[109] of your person in
trial.

Hamlet Sir, I will walk here in the hall. If it please his Majesty, 'tis
165   the breathing time[110] of day with me. Let the foils be
brought. The gentleman willing, and the King hold his
purpose, I will win for him an[111] I can. If not, I will gain
nothing but my shame and the odd[112] hits.

Osric   Shall I deliver you e'en[113] so?

170 Hamlet To this effect, sir, after[114] what flourish your nature will.

Osric   I commend[115] my duty to your lordship.

103 to continue
104 bouts
105 outdo you by
106 determination, test
107 give
108 what
109 offering for combat
110 exercise time
111 if
112 extra
113 communicate your message/response exactly
114 according to
115 present, give

Hamlet Yours, yours.

EXIT OSRIC

He does well to commend it himself. There are no tongues else
for's turn.[116]

Horatio This lapwing runs away with the shell on his head.[117] 175

Hamlet 'A did comply with his dug,[118] before 'a sucked it. Thus
has he, and many more of the same bevy that I know the
drossy age dotes on, only got the tune[119] of the time and, out
of an habit of encounter, a kind of yeasty collection, which
carries them through and through the most fanned and 180
winnowed[120] opinions. And do but blow them to their trial,
the bubbles are out.[121]

ENTER A LORD

Lord My lord, his Majesty commended him to you by young
Osric, who brings back to him that you attend[122] him in the

---

116 no other voices to speak for his use/purpose (to commend/praise Osric)

117 proverbial: the lapwing is a kind of plover, the newly hatched chick of
which was thought to run about with the top half of the egg still on its
head

118 observe the forms of civility/politeness/courtesy with the nipple of his
nurse's breast

119 company/crowd (primarily used with reference to women) that I know
the scum-filled/rubbish-ridden age dotes on have caught/acquired only
the style/frame of mind

120 out of a settled/habitual/rote way of face-to-face meeting, a kind of
restlessly turbid/frothy/foaming collection/summary, which carries them
from beginning to end/over and over again through the most thoroughly
blown about and sifted

121 blow them to their examination/test/proof, the bubbles are popped/
extinguished

122 await, wait upon

185   hall. He sends to know if your pleasure hold to play[123] with
      Laertes, or that you will take longer time.

Hamlet I am constant to my purposes. They follow the King's
      pleasure. If his fitness speaks,[124] mine is ready, now or
      whensoever, provided I be so able as now.

190 *Lord*   The King and Queen and all are coming down.

Hamlet In happy time.[125]

Lord   The Queen desires you to use some gentle
      entertainment to Laertes before you fall to[126] play.

Hamlet She well instructs me.

EXIT LORD

195 *Horatio* You will lose this wager, my lord.

Hamlet I do not think so. Since he went into France, I have been
      in continual practice. I shall win at the odds. But thou
      wouldst not think how ill all's here about[127] my heart – but it
      is no matter.

200 *Horatio* Nay, good my lord –

Hamlet It is but foolery; but it is such a kind of gain-giving[128] as
      would perhaps trouble a woman.

Horatio If your mind dislike any thing, obey it. I will forestall
      their repair[129] hither, and say you are not fit.[130]

---

123 sport now
124 if his readiness/convenience signals/addresses me
125 at a good/fortunate moment (a conventionally polite phrase)
126 gentle treatment/reception ("courtesy") to Laertes before you pass/move
    into your sport
127 how badly everything feels, here around/near
128 misgiving
129 intercept, their making their way
130 ready, prepared

Hamlet Not a whit. We defy augury.[131] There's a special 205
  providence in the fall of a sparrow.[132] If it[133] be now, 'tis not
  to come. If it be not to come, it will be now. If it be not now,
  yet it will come. The readiness is all. Since no man, of aught
  he leaves, knows aught, what is't to leave betimes? Let be.[134]

ENTER CLAUDIUS, GERTRUDE, LAERTES, LORDS, OSRIC,
AND ATTENDANTS WITH FOILS, &C

Claudius Come, Hamlet, come, and take this hand[135] from me. 210

CLAUDIUS PUTS LAERTES' HAND INTO HAMLET'S

Hamlet   Give me your pardon, sir: I have done you wrong,
  But pardon't, as you are a gentleman.
  This presence[136] knows, and you must needs have heard,
  How I am punished with a sore distraction.[137]
  What I have done 215
  That might your nature,[138] honor and exception
  Roughly awake,[139] I here proclaim was madness.
  Was't Hamlet wronged Laertes? Never Hamlet.
  If Hamlet from himself be ta'en away,
  And when he's not himself does wrong Laertes, 220

131 I reject/renounce/disdain predictions of the future
132 "Are not two sparrows sold for a farthing? And one of them shall not fall
  on the ground without your Father": Matthew 10.29
133 the time of death
134 early/in a short time. Let it be
135 Laertes'
136 this company, those assembled here
137 painful/bitter/grievous/severe mental perturbation/madness
138 inherent human disposition, natural human feeling/affection
139 and disapproval violently rouse/make active

Then Hamlet does it not, Hamlet denies[140] it.
Who does it, then? His madness. If't be so,
Hamlet is of the faction that is wronged:
His madness is poor Hamlet's enemy.
225 Sir, in[141] this audience,
Let my disclaiming from a purposed[142] evil
Free me so far in your most generous thoughts
That[143] I have shot mine arrow o'er the house
And hurt my brother.

Laertes   I am satisfied in nature,
230 Whose motive,[144] in this case, should stir me most
To my revenge. But in my terms of honor
I stand aloof, and will[145] no reconcilement
Till by some elder masters, of known honor,
I have a voice and precedent of peace,
235 To keep my name ungored.[146] But till that time,
I do receive your offered love like love
And will not wrong it.

Hamlet   I embrace it freely;
And will this brothers' wager frankly play.[147]
Give us the foils. Come on.

Laertes   Come, one for me.

140 contradicts, forbids
141 in the presence of
142 let my renouncing of an intentional
143 that it will seem to you as if
144 in natural human feeling/affection, whose motivation
145 I stay/stop at a distance, and want
146 a judgment/opinion and proof that this adheres to tradition/custom (the rules of honor), to keep my name unwounded
147 freely/openly engage in

Hamlet   I'll be your foil, Laertes. In mine ignorance   240
    Your skill shall, like a star i' the darkest night,
    Stick fiery off indeed.[148]

Laertes   You mock me, sir.

Hamlet   No, by this hand.

Claudius Give them the foils, young Osric. Cousin Hamlet,
    You know the wager?

Hamlet   Very well, my lord   245
    Your grace hath laid the odds o' th' weaker side.

Claudius I do not fear it; I have seen you both.
    But since he is bettered,[149] we have therefore odds.[150]

Laertes   This is too heavy. Let me see another.

Hamlet   This likes me well. These foils have all a length?   250

THEY PREPARE TO FENCE

Osric   Ay, my good lord.

Claudius Set me the stoups of wine[151] upon that table.
    If Hamlet give[152] the first or second hit,
    Or quit in answer[153] of the third exchange,
    Let all the battlements their ordnance fire.[154]   255
    The king shall drink to Hamlet's better breath,
    And in the cup an union[155] shall he throw,
    Richer than that which four successive kings

148 project far out indeed
149 improved, grown better
150 Hamlet needs only 9 hits out of 21 for the King to win
151 I wish the tankards/flagons of wine to be set
152 makes
153 balances the score, via a return hit
154 indented parapets/battle stations on top of the castle walls fire their cannon
155 Hamlet's free and easy breathing, and will throw a pearl in the cup

In Denmark's crown have worn. Give me the cups,
260 And let the kettle[156] to the trumpet speak,
The trumpet to the cannoneer without,
The cannons to the heavens, the heavens to earth,
"Now the king drinks to Hamlet." Come, begin.
And you, the judges, bear a wary eye.

265 *Hamlet*   Come on, sir.
Laertes   Come, my lord.

THEY FENCE

Hamlet   One.
Laertes   No.
Hamlet   Judgment.[157]
Osric   A hit, a very palpable[158] hit.
Laertes   Well, again.
Claudius   Stay. Give me drink. Hamlet, this pearl is thine.
Here's to thy health.

TRUMPETS SOUND, AND CANNON SHOT WITHIN

Give him the cup.
270 *Hamlet*   I'll play this bout first. Set it by awhile. Come.

THEY FENCE

Another hit. What say you?
Laertes   A touch, a touch, I do confess't.
Claudius   Our son shall win.

156 kettledrum
157 an appeal to the judge, Osric
158 tangible, patent, readily perceived

Gertrude   He's fat, and scant[159] of breath.

Here, Hamlet, take my napkin,[160] rub thy brows.

The queen carouses to thy fortune, Hamlet.   275

Hamlet   Good madam.

Claudius   Gertrude, do not drink.

Gertrude   I will, my lord. I pray you, pardon me.

SHE DRINKS

Claudius   (aside) It is the poisoned cup. It is too late.

Hamlet   I dare not drink yet, madam. By and by.

Gertrude   Come, let me wipe thy face.   280

Laertes   (aside to King) My lord, I'll hit him now.

Claudius   I do not
think't.

Laertes   (aside) And yet 'tis almost 'gainst my conscience.

Hamlet   Come, for the third, Laertes. You but dally.[161]

I pray you, pass with your best violence.[162]

I am afeard[163] you make a wanton[164] of me.   285

Laertes   Say you so? Come on.

THEY FENCE

Osric   Nothing neither way.

Laertes   Have at you now!

---

159   sweaty/slow (or fat), and short
160   small towel (for table use)
161   third bout, Laertes. You just loiter/fool about
162   thrust/lunge with your greatest force/strength
163   afraid
164   spoiled boy

LAERTES WOUNDS HAMLET; THEN, IN SCUFFLING, THEY
EXCHANGE RAPIERS, AND HAMLET WOUNDS LAERTES

Claudius   Part them. They are incensed.[165]

Hamlet Nay, come. Again!

GERTRUDE FALLS

Osric   Look to[166] the Queen there, ho!

290 *Horatio* They bleed on both sides. How is it,[167] my lord?

Osric How is't, Laertes?

Laertes Why, as a woodcock to mine own springe,[168] Osric.
  I am justly killed with mine own treachery.

Hamlet How does the Queen?

Claudius   She swounds[169] to see them
  bleed.

295 *Gertrude* No, no, the drink, the drink. – O my dear Hamlet! –
  The drink, the drink! I am poisoned.

DIES

Hamlet O villany! Ho! Let the door be locked.
  Treachery! Seek it out.

Laertes It[170] is here,[171] Hamlet. Hamlet, thou art slain.

300 No med'cine in the world can do thee good:

---

165 excited, angry
166 attend to
167 how are you
168 bird in my own trap/snare
169 swoons, faints
170 the treachery Hamlet proposes to seek
171 a gesture is surely associated with this statement: a confession, if Laertes
  points to himself, but a more general accusation if he gestures toward the
  King

In thee there is not half an hour of life.
The treacherous instrument is in thy hand,
Unbated and envenomed. The foul practice[172]
Hath turned itself on me. Lo, here I lie,
Never to rise again. Thy mother's poisoned.   305
I can no more. The King, the King's to blame.

Hamlet   The point envenomed too?
Then venom, to thy work![173]

STABS CLAUDIUS

All   Treason! Treason!
Claudius   O, yet defend me, friends. I am but hurt.[174]   310
Hamlet   Here, thou incestuous, murd'rous, damnèd Dane,
Drink off[175] this potion. Is thy union[176] here?
Follow my mother.

CLAUDIUS DIES

Laertes   He is justly served.
It is a poison tempered[177] by himself.
Exchange forgiveness with me, noble Hamlet.   315
Mine and my father's death come not upon thee,[178]

---

172 its point uncovered/bare and poisoned. The foul trick/scheme
173 Note that Hamlet now knows his mother is poisoned but does not attack
    the King until learning that he himself is poisoned. Nor does he mention
    either his father's or his mother's death as he attacks
174 still protect/guard/uphold me, friends. I am only hurt (not mortally
    wounded)
175 drink the rest of/finish
176 the pearl put there by the King (it has been suggested that "union" also
    alludes to the King's marriage to Gertrude)
177 mixed, blended, prepared
178 may my death and my father's not be charged to you, in heaven

Nor thine on me.

DIES

Hamlet   Heaven make thee free of it.[179] I follow thee.
I am dead, Horatio. Wretched queen, adieu!
320   You that look pale and tremble at this chance,
That[180] are but mutes or audience to this act,
Had I but time – as this fell sergeant,[181] death,
Is strict in his arrest[182] – O, I could tell you –
But let it be. Horatio, I am dead;
325   Thou livest. Report me and my cause aright
To the unsatisfied.[183]
Horatio   Never believe it.
I am more an antique Roman[184] than a Dane.
Here's yet some liquor[185] left.
Hamlet   As th' art a man,
Give me the cup. (*Horatio resists*) Let go. By heaven, I'll ha't!
330   (*Hamlet takes* it) O God, Horatio, what a wounded name,
Things standing thus unknown, shall live behind me!
If thou didst ever hold[186] me in thy heart
Absent thee from felicity[187] awhile,

179 and may heaven make you exempt you from my death
180 at this happening/circumstance, you that
181 since this fierce/ruthless/terrible officer/bailiff
182 stopping of things in motion
183 motives/purposes correctly/justly to those who do not know/who are in
    doubt
184 I am quite prepared to commit suicide
185 containing the fatal poison
186 have
187 happiness, bliss (in heaven)

And in this harsh world draw thy breath in pain,
To tell my story.

              What warlike noise is this?   335

Osric   Young Fortinbras, with conquest come[188] from Poland,
To th' ambassadors of England gives
This warlike volley.

Hamlet   O, I die, Horatio.
The potent poison quite o'er-crows[189] my spirit.
I cannot live to hear the news from England,   340
But I do prophesy th' election lights[190]
On Fortinbras. He has my dying voice.
So tell him, with the occurrents, more and less,
Which have solicited.[191] The rest is silence.

Horatio   Now cracks a noble heart. Good night sweet prince,   345
And flights of angels sing thee to thy rest!
Why does the drum come hither?

Fortinbras Where is[192] this sight?

188 returning victorious from
189 is victorious over (as a fighting cock)
190 to be held in Denmark, now that the king is dead, falls/settles on (*and* –
    figuratively – shines on)
191 the events/details, both major and minor, which have drawn on/called
    them forth
192 from what source is/how did all this happen

Horatio   What is it ye would see?
If aught of woe or wonder,[193] cease your search.

350 *Fortinbras* This quarry cries on havoc.[194] O proud Death,
What feast is toward[195] in thine eternal cell,
That thou so many princes at a shot
So bloodily hast struck?

Ambassador   The sight is dismal,[196]
And our affairs from England come too late.
355 The ears are senseless that should give us hearing,
To tell him his commandment is fulfilled,
That Rosencrantz and Guildenstern are dead.
Where should we have our thanks?

Horatio   Not from his mouth,
Had it the ability of life to thank you.
360 He never gave commandment for their death.
But since, so jump[197] upon this bloody question –
You from the Polack wars, and you from England –
Are here arrived, give order that these bodies
High on a stage[198] be placèd to the view,
365 And let me speak to th' yet unknowing world
How these things came about. So shall you hear
Of carnal,[199] bloody, and unnatural acts,
Of accidental judgments, casual slaughters,[200]

193 astonishment
194 heap/pile of corpses (hunting usage) cries/screams of devastation/
    destruction
195 approaching, impending, in preparation
196 sinister/malign/disastrous
197 exactly, precisely
198 platform, scaffold
199 carnivorous
200 accidental decisions, unplanned slaughters

Of deaths put on by cunning and forced cause,[201]
And, in this upshot, purposes mistook[202]   370
Fall'n on th' inventors'[203] heads. All this can I
Truly deliver.[204]

Fortinbras   Let us haste to hear it,
And call the noblest to the audience.
For me, with sorrow I embrace my fortune.[205]
I have some rights of memory[206] in this kingdom,   375
Which now to claim my vantage doth invite me.[207]

Horatio   Of that I shall have also cause to speak,
And[208] from his mouth whose voice will draw on more.[209]
But let this same be presently performed,[210]
Even while men's minds are wild,[211] lest more mischance   380
On[212] plots and errors happen.

Fortinbras   Let four captains[213]
Bear Hamlet like a soldier to the stage,
For he was likely, had he been put on,
To have proved most royal.[214] And for his passage[215]

---

201 deaths imposed/inflicted by crafty and distorted purposes/reasons
202 and, in this result/conclusion, wrongly conceived/erroneous intentions
203 those who designed these false/fictitious things
204 truthfully utter/state/set forth
205 I adopt/accept my luck
206 some remembered and justifiable legal/moral claims
207 my favorable opportunity/superior position/advantage does attract me
208 reason/motivation/grounds, and to speak of words
209 will lead/influence more voices
210 let this aforesaid thing take place at once/immediately
211 precisely now when men's minds are uncontrolled/violent
212 more disasters concerning
213 a military rank equivalent, in current usage, to "general"
214 pushed forward/elected (to the throne *or* put on as a play [?]), to have
       shown himself appropriately kinglike
215 death ("passage" out of bodily life and into "soul" life)

385   The soldiers' music and the rites of war
       Speak[216] loudly for him.
       Take up the bodies. Such a sight as this
       Becomes the field, but here shows much amiss.[217]
       Go, bid the soldiers shoot.

EXEUNT, BEARING OFF THE DEAD BODIES, AFTER THE WHICH
A PEAL[218] OF ORDNANCE IS SHOT OFF

216 will speak / sound / proclaim
217 befits / belongs on the battlefield, but here appears / seems very faulty / off
     the mark / wrong
218 volley, discharge

The last we see of Hamlet at the court in act 4 is his exit for England:

Hamlet   For England?
Claudius   Ay, Hamlet.
Hamlet   Good.
Claudius So is't, if thou knew'st our purposes.
Hamlet   I see a cherub that sees them. But, come, for
England! Farewell, dear mother.
Claudius Thy loving father, Hamlet.
Hamlet   My mother. Father and mother is man and wife,
man and wife is one flesh – and so: my mother. Come, for
England!

EXIT

It is a critical commonplace to assert that the Hamlet of act 5 is a changed man: mature rather than youthful, certainly quieter, if not quietistic, and somehow more attuned to divinity. Perhaps the truth is that he is at last himself, no longer afflicted by mourning and melancholia, by murderous jealousy and incessant rage. Certainly he is no longer haunted by his father's ghost. It may be that the desire for revenge is fading in him. In all of act 5 he does not speak once of his dead father directly. There is a single reference to "my father's signet," which serves to seal up the doom of those poor schoolfellows, Rosencrantz and Guildenstern, and there is the curious phrasing of "my king" rather than "my father" in the halfhearted rhetorical question the prince addresses to Horatio:

Does it not, think'st thee, stand me now upon –
He that hath killed my king and whored my mother,
Popped in between th' election and my hopes,
Thrown out his angle for my proper life,
And with such coz'nage – is't not perfect conscience
To quit him with this arm?

When Horatio responds that Claudius will hear shortly from England, presumably that Rosencrantz and Guildenstern have been executed, Hamlet rather ambiguously makes what might be read as a final vow of revenge:

It will be short. The interim is mine,
And a man's life's no more than to say "one."

However this is to be interpreted, Hamlet forms no plot, and is content with a wise passivity, knowing that Claudius must act. Except for the scheme of Claudius and Laertes, we and the prince might be confronted by a kind of endless standoff. What seems clear is that the urgency of the earlier Hamlet has gone. Instead, a mysterious and beautiful disinterestedness dominates this truer Hamlet, who compels a universal love precisely because he is beyond it, except for its exemplification by Horatio. What we overhear is an ethos so original that we still cannot assimilate it:

> Sir, in my heart there was a kind of fighting,
> That would not let me sleep. Methought I lay
> Worse than the mutines in the bilboes. Rashly —
> And praised be rashness for it. Let us know
> Our indiscretion sometimes serves us well,
> When our deep plots do pall. And that should teach us
> There's a divinity that shapes our ends,
> Rough-hew them how we will —

Weakly read, that divinity is Jehovah, but more strongly "ends" here are not our intentions but rather our fates, and the contrast is between a force that can *shape* stone, and our wills that only hew roughly against implacable substance. Nor would a strong reading find Calvin in the echoes of the Gospel of Matthew as Hamlet sets aside his own: "Thou wouldst not think how ill all's here about my heart." In his heart, there is again a kind of fighting, but the readiness, rather than the ripeness, is now all:

> Not a whit. We defy augury. There's a special providence in
> the fall of a sparrow. If it be now, 'tis not to come. If it be
> not to come, it will be now. If it be not now, yet it will
> come. The readiness is all. Since no man, of aught he
> leaves, knows aught, what is't to leave betimes? Let be.

The apparent nihilism more than negates the text cited from Matthew, yet the epistemological despair presents itself not as despair but as an achieved serenity. Above all else, these are not the accents of an avenger, or even of someone who still mourns, or who continues to suffer the selfish virtues of the natural heart. Not nihilism but authentic disinterestedness, and yet what is that? No

Elizabethan lore, no reading in Aristotle, or even in Montaigne, can help to answer that question. We know the ethos of disinterestedness only because we know Hamlet. Nor can we hope to know Hamlet any better by knowing Freud. The dead father indeed was, during four acts, more powerful than even the living one could be, but by act 5 the dead father is not even a numinous shadow. He is merely a precursor, Hamlet the Dane before this one, and this one matters much more. The tragic hero in Shakespeare, at his most universally moving, is a representation so original that conceptually *he contains us,* and fashions our psychology of motives permanently. Our map or general theory of the mind may be Freud's, but Freud, like all the rest of us, inherits the representation of mind, at its most subtle and excellent, from Shakespeare. Freud could say that the aim of all life was death, but not that readiness is all.

Originality in regard to Shakespeare is a bewildering notion, because we have no rival to set him against. "The originals are not original," Emerson liked to remark, but he withdrew that observation in respect to Shakespeare. If Shakespeare had a direct precursor it had to be Marlowe, who was scarcely six months older. Yet, in comparison to Shakespeare, Marlowe represents persons only by caricature. The Chaucer who could give us the Pardoner or the Wife of Bath appears to be Shakespeare's only authentic English precursor, if we forget the English renderings of the Bible. Yet we do not take our psychology from Chaucer or even from the Bible. Like Freud himself, we owe our psychology to Shakespeare. Before Shakespeare, representations in literature may change *as* they speak, but they do not change *because* of what they say. Shakespearean representation turns upon his persons listening to themselves simultaneously with our listening, and learning and changing even as we learn and change. Falstaff delights himself as much as he delights us, and Hamlet modifies himself by studying his own modifications. Ever since, Falstaff has been the inescapable model for nearly all wit, and Hamlet the paradigm for all introspection. When Yorick's skull replaces the helmeted ghost, then the mature Hamlet has replaced the self-chastising revenger, and a different sense of death's power over life has been created, and in more than a play or a dramatic poem:

> *Hamlet* To what base uses we may return, Horatio! Why may
>   not imagination trace the noble dust of Alexander, till he
>   find it stopping a bung-hole?
> *Horatio* 'Twere to consider too curiously, to consider so.
> *Hamlet* No, faith, not a jot, but to follow him thither with
>   modesty enough, and likelihood to lead it.

Probability leads possibility, likelihood beckons imagination on, and Alexander is essentially a surrogate for the dead father, the Danish Alexander. Passionately reductive, Hamlet would consign his own dust to the same likelihood, but there we part from him, with Horatio as our own surrogate. Hamlet's unique praise of Horatio sets forever the paradigm of the Shakespearean reader or playgoer in relation to the Shakespearean tragic hero:

> Dost thou hear?
> Since my dear soul was mistress of her choice
> And could of men distinguish her election,
> S' hath sealed thee for herself, for thou hast been
> As one, in suff'ring all, that suffers nothing,

Which means, not that Horatio and the reader do not suffer with Hamlet, but rather that truly they suffer nothing precisely because they learn from Hamlet the disinterestedness they themselves cannot exemplify, though in possibility somehow share. And they survive, to tell Hamlet's story "of accidental judgments" not so accidental and perhaps not judgments, since disinterestedness does not judge, and there are no accidents.

Only Hamlet, at the last, is disinterested, since the hero we see in act 5, despite his protestations, is now beyond love, which is not to say that he never loved Gertrude, or Ophelia, or the dead father, or poor Yorick for that matter. Hamlet is an actor? Yes, earlier, but not in act 5, where he has ceased also to be a play director, and finally even abandons the profession of poet. Language, so dominant as such in the earlier Hamlet, gives almost the illusion of transparency in his last speech, if only because he verges upon saying what cannot be said:

> You that look pale and tremble at this chance,
> That are but mutes or audience to this act,
> Had I but time – as this fell sergeant, death,
> Is strict in his arrest – O, I could tell you –
> But let it be.

Evidently he does know something of what he leaves, and we ache to know what he could tell us, since it is Shakespeare's power to persuade us that Hamlet has gained a crucial knowledge. One clue is the abiding theatrical trope of "but mutes or audience," which suggests that the knowledge is itself "of" illusion. But the trope is framed by two announcements to Horatio and so to us – "I am dead" – and no other figure in Shakespeare seems to stand so authoritatively on the threshold between the worlds of life and death. When the hero's last speech moves between "O, I die, Horatio" and "the rest is silence," there is a clear sense again that much more might be said, concerning our world and not the "undiscovered country" of death. The hint is that Hamlet could tell us something he has learned about the nature of representation, because he has learned what it is that he himself represents.

Shakespeare gives Fortinbras the last word on this, but that word is irony, since Fortinbras represents only the formula of repetition: like father, like son. "The soldier's music and the rite of war" speak loudly for the dead father, but not for this dead son, who had watched the army of Fortinbras march past to gain its little patch of ground and had mused that: "Rightly to be great / Is not to stir without great argument." The reader's last word has to be Horatio's, who more truly than Fortinbras has Hamlet's dying voice: "And from his mouth whose voice will draw on more," which only in a minor key means draw more supporters to the election of Fortinbras. Horatio represents the audience, while Fortinbras represents all the dead fathers.

We love Hamlet, then, for whatever reasons Horatio loves him. Of Horatio we know best that what distinguishes him from Rosencrantz and Guildenstern, and indeed from Polonius, Ophelia, Laertes, and Gertrude, is that Claudius *cannot use him*. Critics have remarked upon Horatio's ambiguously shifting status at the court of Denmark, and the late William Empson confessed a certain irritation at Hamlet's discovery of virtues in Horatio that the prince could not find in himself. Yet Shakespeare gives us a Hamlet we must love while knowing our inferiority, since he has the qualities we lack, and so he also gives us Horatio, our representative, who loves so stoically for the rest of us. Horatio is loyal, and limited; skeptical as befits a fellow student of the profoundly skeptical Hamlet, yet never skeptical about Hamlet. Take Horatio out of the play, and you take us out of the play. The plot could be rearranged to spare the wretched Rosencrantz and Guildenstern, even to spare Laertes, let alone Fortinbras, but remove Horatio, and Hamlet becomes so estranged from us that we scarcely can hope to account for that universality of appeal which is his, and the play's, most original characteristic.

Horatio, then, represents by way of our positive association with him; it is a commonplace, but not less true for that, to say that Hamlet represents by negation. I think this negation is biblical in origin, which is why it seems so Freudian to us, because Freudian negation is biblical and not Hegelian, as it were. Hamlet is biblical rather than Homeric or Sophoclean. Like the Hebrew hero confronting Yahweh, Hamlet needs to be everything in himself yet knows the sense in which he is nothing in himself. What Hamlet takes back from repression is returned only cognitively, never affectively, so that in him thought is liberated from its sexual past, but at the high expense of a continued and augmenting sense of sexual disgust. And what Hamlet at first loves is what biblical and Freudian man loves: the image of authority, the dead father, and the object of the dead father's love, who is also the object of Claudius's love. When Hamlet matures, or returns fully to himself, he transcends the love of authority, and ceases to love at all, and perhaps he can be said to be dying throughout all of act 5, and not just in the scene of the duel.

In Freud, we love authority, but authority does not love us in return. Nowhere in the play are we told, by Hamlet or by anyone else, of the love of the dead king for his son, but only for Gertrude. That Hamlet hovers always beyond our comprehension must be granted, yet he is not so far beyond as to cause us to see him with the vision of Fortinbras, rather than the vision of Horatio. We think of him not necessarily as royal, but more as noble, in the archaic sense of "noble," which is to be a seeing soul. It is surely no accident that Horatio is made to emphasize the word "noble" in his elegy for Hamlet, which contrasts angelic song to "the soldier's music" of Fortinbras. As a noble or seeing heart, Hamlet indeed sees feelingly. Short of T. S. Eliot's judgment that the play is an aesthetic failure, the oddest opinion in the *Hamlet* criticism of our time was that of W. H. Auden in his Ibsen essay, "Genius and Apostle," which contrasts Hamlet as a mere actor to Don Quixote as the antithesis of an actor:

> Hamlet lacks faith in God and in himself. Consequently he must define his existence in terms of others, e.g., I am the man whose mother married his uncle who murdered his father. He would like to become what the Greek tragic hero is, a creature of situation. Hence his inability to act, for he can only "act," i.e., play at possibilities.

Harold Goddard, whose *The Meaning of Shakespeare* (1951) seems to me still the most illuminating single book on Shakespeare, remarked that "Hamlet is his own Falstaff." In Goddard's spirit, I might venture the formula that Brutus plus Falstaff equals Hamlet, though "equals" is hardly an accurate word here. A better formula was proposed by A. C. Bradley, when he suggested that Hamlet was the only Shakespearean character whom we could think had written Shakespeare's plays. Goddard built on this by saying of Shakespeare: "He is an unfallen Hamlet." From a scholarly or any formalist perspective, Goddard's aphorism is not criticism, but neither historical research nor formalist modes of criticism have helped us much in learning to describe the unassimilated originality that Shakespearean representation still constitutes. Because we are formed by Shakespeare, paradoxically most fully where we cannot assimilate him, we are a little blinded by what might be called the originality of this originality. Only a few critics (A. D. Nuttall among them) have seen that the central element in this originality is its cognitive power. Without Shakespeare (and the Bible as his precursor text) we would not know of a literary representation that worked so as to compel "reality" (be it Platonic or Humean, Hegelian or Freudian) to reveal aspects of itself we previously could not discern. Such a representation cannot be considered antimimetic or an effect of language alone.

One way, by no means unproductive, of accounting for the force of Shakespearean representation is to see it as the supreme instance of what the late Paul de Man called a poetics of modernity, of a revisionism of older literary conventions that at once subsumed and canceled the illusions always present in all figurative language. Howard Felperin, working in de Man's mode, adroitly reads Macbeth's "modernity" as the dilemma of a figure totally unable to take his own nature for granted: "He cannot quite rest content in an action in which his role and his nature are determined in advance, but must continuously reinvent himself in the process of acting them out." In such a view, Macbeth is a strong misreading of a figure like Herod in the old morality plays. I would go further and suggest that the drama *Macbeth* is an allusive triumph over more formidable precursors, just as *King Lear* is. The Shakespearean Sublime, too strong to find agonists in Seneca or in the native tradition (even in Marlowe), and too remote from Athenian drama to feel its force, confronts instead the Sublime of the Bible. What breaks loose in the apocalyptic cosmos of *Macbeth* or of *Lear* is an energy of the abyss or the original chaos that is ignored in the priestly first chapter of

Genesis, but which wars fiercely against Jehovah in crucial passages of Job, the Psalms, and Isaiah. To subsume and supersede the Bible could not have been the conscious ambition of Shakespeare, but if we are to measure the preternatural energies of *Macbeth* or of *Lear,* then we will require Job or Isaiah or certain Psalms as the standard of measurement.

What is the advance, cognitive and figurative, that Shakespearean representation achieves over biblical depiction? The question is absurdly difficult, yet anything but meaningless. If Shakespeare has a true Western rival, then he is either the Yahwist, the Hebrew Bible's great original, or the Homer of the *Iliad.* Can there *be* an advance over Jacob or Achilles as representations of reality, whatever that is taken to be? What the question reduces to is the unanswerable: can there be advances in reality? The arts, as Hazlitt insisted, are not progressive, and if reality is, then its progression suspiciously resembles a speeding up of what Freud called the death drive. Reality testing, like the reality principle, is Freud's only transcendentalism, his last vestige of Platonism. Freud's own originality, as he deeply sensed, tends to evaporate when brought too near either to the originality of the Yahwist or to the originality of Shakespeare. This may be the true cause of the disaster that is *Moses and Monotheism,* and of Freud's own passion for the lunatic thesis that Shakespeare's plays were written by the earl of Oxford.

By Nietzsche's genealogical test for the memorable, which is cognitive pain, Job is no more nor less forgettable than *Macbeth* or *Lear.* The rhetorical economy of Job's wife, in her one appearance, unmatchable even out of context, is overwhelming within context, and may have set for Shakespeare one of the limits of representation:

So went Satan forth from the presence of the Lord, and smote Job with sore boils from the sole of his foot unto his crown.

And he took him a potsherd to scrape himself withal; and he sat down among the ashes.

Then said his wife unto him, Dost thou still retain thine integrity? Curse God, and die.

Lear's Queen, the mother of Goneril, Regan, and Cordelia, had she survived to accompany her husband onto the heath, hardly could have said more in less. In Shakespeare's tragedies there are moments of compressed urgency that represent uncanny yet persuasive change with biblical economy. The dying Edmund sees the bodies of Goneril and Regan brought in, and belatedly turns his lifetime about in four words: "Yet Edmund was belov'd." The phrase is a vain attempt to countermand his own order for the murder of Cordelia. "Yet Edmund was belov'd" — though loved by two fiends, the shock of knowing he *was* loved, unto death, undoes "mine own nature." One thinks of Hamlet's "Let be" that concludes his "We defy augury" speech, as he goes into the trap of Claudius's last plot. "Let be" epitomizes what I have called "disinterestedness," though Horatio's word "noble" may be more apt. That laconic "Let be," repeated as "Let it be" in Hamlet's death speech, is itself a kind of catastrophe creation, even as it marks another phase in Hamlet's release from what Freud called the family romance, and even as it compels another transference for our veneration to Hamlet. Catastrophe creation, family romance, transference: these are the stigmata and consequently the paradigms for imaginative originality in the Bible and, greatly shadowed, in Freud, and I suggest now that they can be useful paradigms for the apprehension of originality in Shakespeare's tragic representations. The fantasy of rescuing the mother from degradation is palpable in Hamlet; less palpable and far more revelatory is the sense in which the prince has molded himself into a pragmatic changeling. The ghost is armed for war, and Hamlet, grappling with Laertes in the graveyard, accurately warns Laertes (being to that extent his father's son) that as the prince he has something dangerous in him. But is Hamlet psychically ever armed for war? Claudius, popping in between the election and Hamlet's hopes, could have shrewdly pled more than his nephew's youth and inexperience while properly arguing that his own nature was better qualified for the throne. Hamlet, in the graveyard, shocked back from beyond affect, accurately indicates whose true son he first became as changeling:

> Alas, poor Yorick! I knew him, Horatio – a fellow of infi-
> nite jest, of most excellent fancy. He hath bore me on his
> back a thousand times. And now how abhorred in my
> imagination it is! My gorge rises at it. Here hung those
> lips that I have kissed I know not how oft.

Harry Levin, for whom strong misreading is not serendipity but misfortune, advises us that "Hamlet without *Hamlet* has been thought about all too much." One might reply, in all mildness, that little memorable has been written about *Hamlet* that does not fall into the mode of "Hamlet without *Hamlet*." Far more even than *Lear* or *Macbeth,* the play is the figure; the question of *Hamlet* only can be Hamlet. He does not move in a Sublime cosmos, and truly has no world except himself, which would appear to be what he has learned in the interim between acts 4 and 5. Changelings who move from fantasy to fact are possible only in romance, and alas Shakespeare wrote the tragedy of Hamlet, and not the romance of Hamlet instead. But the originality of Shakespearean representation in tragedy, and particularly in *Hamlet,* hardly can be overstressed. Shakespeare's version of the family romance always compounds it with two other paradigms for his exuberant originality: with a catastrophe that creates and with a carrying across from earlier ambivalences within the audience to an ambivalence that is a kind of taboo settling in about the tragic hero like an aura. At the close of *Hamlet,* only Horatio and Fortinbras are survivors. Fortinbras presumably will be another warrior-king of Denmark. Horatio does not go home with us, but vanishes into the aura of Hamlet's afterlight, perhaps to serve as witness of Hamlet's story over and over again. The hero leaves us with a sense that finally he has fathered himself, that he was beyond our touch though not beyond our affections, and that the catastrophes he helped provoke have brought about, not a new creation, but a fresh revelation of what was latent in reality but not evident without his own disaster.

As a coda, I return to my earlier implication that Shakespearean originality is the consequence of diction or a will over language changing his characters, and not of language itself. More than any other writer, Shakespeare is able to exemplify how meaning gets started rather than just renewed. Auden remarked that Falstaff is free of the superego; there is no over-I or above-I for that triumph of wit. Nietzsche, attempting to represent a man without a superego, gave us Zarathustra, a mixed achievement in himself, but a very poor representation when read side by side with Falstaff. Falstaff or Zarathustra? No conceivable reader would choose the Nietzschean rather than the Shakespearean over-man. Falstaff indeed *is* how meaning gets started: by excess, overflow, emanation, contamination, the will to life. Zarathustra is a juggler of perspectives, a receptive will to interpretation. Poor Falstaff ends in tragedy; his catastrophe is his dreadfully authentic love for Hal. Zarathustra loves only a trope, the solar trajectory, and essentially is himself a trope; he is Nietzsche's metalepsis or transumption of the philosophical tradition. A formalist critic would say that Falstaff is a trope also, a gorgeous and glowing hyperbole. Say rather that Falstaff is a representation, in himself, of how meaning gets started, of how invention is accomplished and manifested. But we remember Falstaff as we want to remember him, triumphant in the tavern, and not rejected in the street. We remember Hamlet as he wanted us to remember him, as Horatio remembers him, without having to neglect his end. Perhaps Hamlet is a representation, in himself, not just of how meaning gets started, but also of how meaning itself is invention, of how meaning refuses to be deferred or to be ended. Perhaps again that is why we can imagine Hamlet as the author of *Hamlet,* as the original we call Shakespeare.

FURTHER READING

General

Bergeron, David M., and Geraldo U. de Sousa. *Shakespeare: A Study and Research Guide.* 3d ed. Lawrence: University Press of Kansas, 1995.

Boyce, Charles. *Shakespeare A to Z: The Essential Reference to His Plays, His Poems, His Life and Times, and More.* New York: Facts on File, 1990.

Bradley, A. C. *Shakespearian Tragedy: Lectures on "Hamlet," "Othello," "King Lear," "Macbeth."* London: Macmillan, 1961.

Colie, Rosalie L. *Shakespeare's Living Art.* Princeton, N.J.: Princeton University Press, 1974.

Dean, Leonard F., ed. *Shakespeare: Modern Essays in Criticism.* Rev. ed. London: Oxford University Press, 1967.

Furness, Horace Howard, ed. *"Hamlet": The New Variorum Edition.* 2 vols. Mineola, N.Y.: Dover, 2000.

Goddard, Harold C. *The Meaning of Shakespeare.* 2 vols. Chicago: University of Chicago Press, 1951.

Gottschalk, Paul. *The Meanings of "Hamlet": Modes of Literary Interpretation Since Bradley.* Albuquerque: University of New Mexico Press, 1972.

Gurr, Andrew. *Playgoing in Shakespeare's London.* Cambridge: Cambridge University Press, 1987.

———. *The Shakespearean Stage, 1574–1642.* 3d ed. Cambridge: Cambridge University Press, 1992.

Halliday, F. E. *The Life of Shakespeare.* London: Duckworth, 1964.

———. *A Shakespeare Companion.* Rev. ed. London: Duckworth, 1977.

Holmes, Martin. *Shakespeare and His Players.* New York: Scribner, 1972.

McDonald, Russ. *The Bedford Companion to Shakespeare: An Introduction with Documents.* Boston: Bedford Books of St. Martin's Press, 1996.

Onions, C. T. *A Shakespeare Glossary.* Enlarged and revised by Robert D. Eagleson. Oxford: Clarendon Press, 1986.

Raffel, Burton. *From Stress to Stress: An Autobiography of English Prosody.* Hamden, Conn.: Archon, 1992.

———. "*Hamlet* and the Tradition of the Novel." *Explorations in Renaissance Culture* 21 (1996): 31–50.

Salgádo, Gámini. *Eyewitnesses of Shakespeare: First Hand Accounts of Performances, 1590–1890.* New York: Barnes and Noble, 1975.

Santillana, Giorgio de, and Hertha von Dechend. *Hamlet's Mill: An Essay on Myth and the Frame of Time.* Boston: Godine, 1977.

Schoenbaum, S. *William Shakespeare: A Compact Documentary Life.* Oxford: Oxford University Press, 1977.

———. *Shakespeare's Lives.* New ed. Oxford: Oxford University Press, 1991.

Stanislavsky, Konstantin. "On *Hamlet.*" In *Shakespeare in the Soviet Union.* Edited by Roman Samarin and Alexander Nikolyukin. Translated by Avril Pyman. Moscow: Institute of World Literature, 1966.

Taylor, Gary. *Reinventing Shakespeare: A Cultural History, from the Restoration to the Present.* New York: Weidenfeld and Nicholson, 1989.

Van Doren, Mark. *Shakespeare.* New York: H. Holt, 1939.

Wells, Stanley. *Shakespeare: A Life in Drama.* New York: W. W. Norton, 1995.

———, ed. *The Cambridge Companion to Shakespeare Studies.* Cambridge: Cambridge University Press, 1986.

Advanced

The Compact Edition of the Oxford English Dictionary: Complete Text Reproduced Micrographically. 2 vols. Glasgow: Oxford University Press, 1971.

Everett, Barbara. *Young Hamlet: Essays on Shakespeare's Tragedies.* Oxford: Oxford University Press, 1989.

Hinman, Charlton. *The First Folio of Shakespeare.* 2d ed. Introduction by Peter W. M. Blayney. New York: W. W. Norton, 1996.

Honigmann, E. A. J. *Shakespeare: The "Lost Years."* 2d ed. Manchester: Manchester University Press, 1998.

Ingram, William. *The Business of Playing: The Beginnings of the Adult Professional Theater in Elizabethan London.* Ithaca, N.Y.: Cornell University Press, 1992.

Jardine, Lisa. *Reading Shakespeare Historically.* London: Routledge, 1996.

Lanham, Richard A. *The Motives of Eloquence: Literary Rhetoric in the Renaissance.* New Haven and London: Yale University Press, 1976.

Laroque, François. *Shakespeare's Festive World: Elizabethan Seasonal Entertainment and the Professional Stage.* Translated by Janet Lloyd. Cambridge: Cambridge University Press, 1991.

Parrott, Thomas Marc, and Hardin Craig, eds. *The Tragedy of "Hamlet": A Critical Edition of the Second Quarto, 1604.* Princeton, N.J.: Princeton University Press, 1938.

Shakespeare's "Hamlet": The Second Quarto. San Marino, Calif.: Huntington Library, 1964.

Thomson, Peter. *Shakespeare's Professional Career.* Cambridge: Cambridge University Press, 1992.

Trousdale, Marion. *Shakespeare and the Rhetoricians.* Chapel Hill: University of North Carolina Press, 1982.

Weimann, Robert. *Shakespeare and the Popular Tradition in the Theater: Studies in the Social Dimension of Dramatic Form and Function.* Edited by Robert Schwartz. Baltimore: Johns Hopkins University Press, 1978.

Weiner, Albert B., ed. *"Hamlet": The First Quarto, 1603.* Foreword by Hardin Craig. Great Neck, N.Y.: Barron's, 1962.

Wells, Stanley, and Gary Taylor, eds. *William Shakespeare: The Complete Works.* Oxford: Clarendon Press, 1993.

FINDING LIST

'a	6, n28	mark	6, n29
affair	23, n98	marry	32, n57
anon	84, n257	matter	65, n46
charge	6, n37	meet	47, n65
corse	19, n57	methink	23, n104
cousin	17, n35	particular	7, n48
doubt	27, n131	passeth	18, n51
dread	16, n26	presently	91, n333
ere	21, n82	stand	3, n1
fair	6, n33	state	9, n82
fantasy	5, n15	stay	6, n39
gentle	20, n65	still	11, n102
habit	31, n50	touching	32, n56
haply	80, n199	very	62, n21
honest	49, n73	wax	28, n11
husbandry	32, n53	wit	64, n44